CAREER ANCHORS
REIMAGINED

EDGAR H. SCHEIN | JOHN VAN MAANEN | PETER A. SCHEIN

CAREER ANCHORS
REIMAGINED

FINDING DIRECTION AND OPPORTUNITY IN THE CHANGING WORLD OF WORK

WILEY

Published by John Wiley & Sons, Inc., Hoboken, New Jersey.
Published simultaneously in Canada.

For general information on our other products and services or for technical support, please contact our Customer Care Department within the United States at (800) 762-2974, outside the United States at (317) 572-3993 or fax (317) 572-4002.

Wiley also publishes its books in a variety of electronic formats. Some content that appears in print may not be available in electronic formats. For more information about Wiley products, visit our web site at www.wiley.com.

Library of Congress Cataloging-in-Publication Data:

Names: Schein, Edgar H., author. | Van Maanen, John, author. | Schein, Peter A., author. | John Wiley & Sons, publisher.
Title: Career anchors reimagined: finding direction and opportunity in the changing world of work / Edgar H. Schein, John Van Maanen, Peter A. Schein.
Description: 5th edition. | Hoboken, New Jersey : Wiley, [2023] | Includes bibliographical references and index.
Identifiers: LCCN 2022047983 (print) | LCCN 2022047984 (ebook) | ISBN 9781119899488 (hardback) | ISBN 9781119899501 (adobe pdf) | ISBN 9781119899495 (epub)
Subjects: LCSH: Vocational guidance.
Classification: LCC HF5381 .S3465 2023 (print) | LCC HF5381 (ebook) | DDC 331.702—dc23/eng/20230109
LC record available at https://lccn.loc.gov/2022047983
LC ebook record available at https://lccn.loc.gov/2022047984

Cover Design: Wiley
Cover Images: © Oliver Hoffmann/Shutterstock, © VMCgroup/Shutterstock

SKY10043073_022123

A Letter To the Reader

It is with heavy hearts that we relay the news to you that Edgar Schein passed away on January 26, 2023, just shy of his 95th birthday. Ed, John, and Peter had just completed the final edits for the book you hold in your hands, *Career Anchors Reimagined*.

A legend in the fields of organizational culture, organization change, and career dynamics, Ed was a brilliant and treasured expert whose work and teachings will long be remembered by those of us at who were fortunate to have worked with him over the years.

Ed was clear, direct, passionate, and thoughtful, and always expressed appreciation of and interest in others. A prolific thinker and author, Ed wrote or cowrote nearly 200 articles and books—many of those with Wiley—over the course of his career. The tremendous impact that his work has had on the lives and livelihoods of others will be felt for year and years to come and we will miss him dearly at Wiley.

Contents

Acknowledgments

WE CAN NEVER go far enough in acknowledging the support of all of our family members who endure the moody distractions of writers writing. In this case we must go farther still to recognize how much children and grandchildren have informed and motivated the writing of this new book. The stories we have heard from twenty-somethings through to fifty-somethings about their career journeys keep us honest, grounded, and inspired. Many of these stories are included, with modifications for our subjects' privacy and also for the *Career Anchors* message. We hope our families feel how much we appreciate their contributions.

We remain deeply indebted to the original panelists whose career paths led to *Career Dynamics* (1978) and all editions of *Career Anchors*. It was, after all, their experiences that were distilled into the eight career patterns later to be described as the eight anchors, still in play today. The importance of longitudinal studies cannot be overstated when thinking about careers. Very little about a career can

ix

be captured in a snapshot. You need to see the motion picture to see the patterns. The panelists who agreed to remain as panelists helped make this good research and helped the authors come up with some ways to guide other career seekers over the many years since.

In addition to the original panelists, we must also pay homage to the numerous students, professionals, practitioners of sundry trades, career counselors, consultants, and assorted other card-carrying members of the helping occupations in and out of organizations who have both used and passed on the ideas conveyed by *Career Anchors*. We have certainly benefited from unfettered responses from many of those who were exposed initially to *Career Anchors* in the classroom, training sessions, career workshops, independently online, by text, or word of mouth. Indeed, such reactions have led to the progressive reshaping of our ideas and models as presented in this book.

Lastly, we want to acknowledge each other. Ed and John have written together before. Peter showed up late to work with us on this one. It's not a foregone conclusion that three people will be able to sit down and write a new book together. These three authors who worked well together as a group hereby pat each other on the back in thanks for not allowing this process to be excruciating and forgettable, and instead, for making this new work exciting and fruitful.

Peter Schein
John Van Maanen
Ed Schein

Preface

Career Anchors in the 21st Century

This 5th edition of *Career Anchors* breaks new ground. While the previous editions clearly captured the 20th century world of work, we think the arc of this century has launched us into some new directions that we can already observe and compel us to reexamine and reset our thinking.

VUCAA

We were, are, and will be in a period of VUCA (Volatility, Uncertainty, Complexity, and Ambiguity). This has been our condition most of the last few decades. And that was before the Covid-19 pandemic made VUCA seem quaint.

As we are writing this edition, the world is facing an uncertain pandemic recovery, a "great resignation" and "quiet quitting", autocratic challenges to an assumed democratic order in many societies, generationally high levels of inflation, inexorable global warming threatening life and work, not to mention grave concerns for much of Western Europe as Russia continues its imperial expansion into Ukraine.

All of these challenges, and no doubt others, suggest to us that we are in an extraordinarily anxious period, hence we add a second "A," *Anxiety*, to the term VUCA. We'll call it *VUCAA* or *VUCA-squared*.

With this anxiety compounding such unsettledness, it is no longer possible to think of "career anchors" in the same ways as suggested by the previous editions. The concept of career itself has a different meaning in our VUCAA context.

Vocational or professional progress, a steady course of accomplishment in a focused domain, may hold true for many. And yet the other sense of the word "career," hurdling along at high speed, where it may be more about the pace than the course, fits the experience of many younger 21st-century employees and entrepreneurs.

When *Career Anchors* was first written the notion of "gig" work may have been thought of as undesired "marginal temp work" or a place for someone who has "trouble holding down a job." Today "gig work" may be thought of as a respectable adaptation to volatile job market conditions, if not an absolute preference for an unencumbered immediate future. Regardless, the pace of change is the feature, not the bug.

This is a different sense of career. A contemporary concept of career must necessarily include experimentation, adaptation, flexibility, opportunism more than dogged "stick-to-it-iveness."

Different Kinds of Anchors

In early *Career Anchors* editions, there was an emphasis on that single, stable center or fulcrum that guided work choices over time. With this edition we abandon that singularity to emphasize what has always been true but underplayed in our previous writings. We now sense that it is not particularly accurate nor helpful to think in terms of *an anchor* compared to thinking of a pattern of preferences reflected in what job decisions we have made, which helps guide what job optimizations we have and would like to make.

At risk of extending a nautical metaphor too far, we might think of the 21st-century anchor as a sea anchor or drogue. In this context, the anchor allows for direction and stability without stopping movement.

What we need is a sea anchor or drogue to keep from being broad-sided by a new trend, a merger, or a reduction in force, and we can only hope the sea anchor provides us some stability to keep us from crashing into the "rocks on shore" such as a bad career choice or a "toxic" work environment.

In our work lives, strong tailwinds may be just as hard to manage as strong headwinds. In either direction, the metaphorical sea anchor or drogue offers comfort and stability while allowing us to steer and optimize our course.

Going forward, career anchors should be thought of as leanings or preferences that will steady us and may change over time—there is nothing cast iron or buried deep about them. They provide stability in tumult and motivation in uncertainty. They do not stop us from exploring, experimenting, and weathering the storm.

Modernizing the Original Research

The pattern of decisions made at key junctures in our past work and life situations helps us understand our anchors. This was the point when *Career Anchors* was first published. All editions of *Career Anchors* are informed by the original research conducted with a panel of mid-career participants.

This research was a longitudinal study over 30 years. Looking back in time, this panel of 20th-century participants presented pretty clear evidence of professional optimization around a central bias among eight dimensions. The reason we are resetting now *is not* that we are abandoning that research at that time but that so much has changed in the job market two decades into the 21st century.

We see *more volatility*—for example, "five jobs in three years" is not an uncommon pattern for twenty-somethings.

We see *more uncertainty*—for example, employment "at will" provides infinite freedom to leave or be terminated as a normal course of business.

We see *more complexity*—for example, dual-career, multiple job households are the norm, not the anomaly.

We see *more ambiguity*—for example, work norms around dress and decorum vary as wildly as do expectations of when and where to get the work done ("9 to 5" is so last century!).

And lastly, we see *more anxiety* about integrating life and work as a function of the aforementioned changes, profoundly increased by working from home, Covid-19 lockdowns, and exhausting videoconferencing as the best we can do to convene and collaborate while working.

A New Visual: The Spiderweb

In the pages that follow, we will revisit the eight anchors and adapt our definitions of them to reflect the work and life changes we see and feel today. Similarly, we will suggest a new metaphor that allows the eight leanings, or factors to be traded off each other, to be seen in their dynamic context in relation to each other.

This new metaphor is the "spiderweb." Eight dimensions on the spiderweb or "radar chart" provide for a visualization of the importance of certain anchors relative to less important anchors. A visible comparison among the eight anchors is now possible and is detailed and illustrated further on in this edition.

We think this visualization fits better in our *VUCAA* world. There is no right answer nor is there one singular answer.

This book is intended to provide insight and self-awareness. It will be up to you to come up with your answers. And even that might be too much to expect. What we do know is that this book will help you tackle tough work-life decisions because you will have an image, a visual, of *what is more and what is less* important.

~ Peter Schein, John Van Maanen, and Ed Schein
Summer 2022

Introduction: Plan for This Book

Dr Seuss:
"You have brains in your head
You have feet in your shoes,
You can steer yourself
Any direction you choose"

WE START WITH the timeless inspiration of Dr. Seuss, Theodore Geisel, from his playful yet profound "career" book *Oh, the Places You'll Go* (Seuss, 1990; New York: Random House). Each chapter except the last will start with an excerpt from Dr. Seuss to help set the table and remind us of the ups and downs of career journeys.

Our goal is to provide you an opportunity to think about your work life and your relationships as you look ahead into a post-pandemic, environmentally challenged new world. We believe that you need to do this thinking because things are dramatically different now as the next chapter will highlight.

We have organized the material for you to analyze your situation and to enable you to identify choices that you may already have made or that will soon be forced upon you by the rapidly evolving economic, social, political, and climate challenges that are all around us and are picking up speed.

Chapter One highlights many of those changes to help you think which of them you have observed and which of them have especially affected you.

Chapter Two asks you to do a deep dive into your various relationships at work, at home, and in your overall life. We will ask you to identify whom you relate to and how deep those various relationships are now and possibly need to be in the future. This will enable a new and more refined view of how you see yourself in relation to work, to family and friends, and to your own self-development. This builds on what in previous editions was called "Job Role Analysis."

Chapter Three reviews our model of the career as having an *external* meaning in terms of the formal or expected steps needed to succeed in a given occupation which we called the "external career." We differentiate this external career from how you learn from your various job experiences what are your competencies, motives, and values. This becomes akin to your self-image or work identity and represents your "internal career."

Chapter Four describes the eight career anchors, which make up some of the main components of that internal career. You are invited to begin to think about how well any of them fit you now or depict where you want to go as you look ahead. To help you do this we provide both formal descriptions and case examples of each anchor.

Chapter Five continues the deep dive into your internal career by asking you to review your job history, in an "interview," preferably with a friend or partner, to analyze how your internal career developed and shaped itself in terms of the various possible anchor categories.

Chapter Six then takes you online and provides you with a 32-item survey that asks you to think about past and future choices and shows you on a "spiderweb" chart your own biases and preferences for the different anchor categories.

Chapter Seven will lead you to a new set of items with which you can identify possible areas of growth as you look ahead into this VUCAA world in terms of the same "spiderweb" chart. This analysis will lead you to a new set of actions based on the confidence that you now know better who you are and what you need to do next.

Chapter Eight presents five detailed *Career Anchors and Growth Intentions* stories, which include completed charts that show the growth intentions alongside the career anchors. These stories highlight the complexities of what you now face and how five career seekers have set their courses in these challenging conditions.

In Chapter Nine we conclude with a step back and reflection on the choices we make along the way.

The Appendix and Bibliography link this edition to the vast literature of research and practice on careers that has arisen in the last fifty years. In the Appendix, we compare *Career Anchors* as a concept with two other very popular career concepts, the CliftonStrengths Assessment and the Myers-Briggs Type Indicator (MBTI) to show both the similarities in these approaches and also to highlight the differences. In the Bibliography, we provide the reader who wants to know more about the research base for this work and what else to read with an extensive list of other publications bearing on mid-life career issues and changes in our work and organizational worlds.

The main body of the text is designed to GET YOU DIRECTLY INVOLVED in thinking about your work and your relationships in this turbulent post-pandemic time— What is happening out there, what is your situation now, and, as you look ahead, what choices confront you?

A Cautionary Note:

Now that you know the arc of this book you may be tempted to skip chapters and to go straight to the two online assessments. You may of course do that, yet we built into Chapter Two important sections on relationships because we feel strongly that relationships will matter more than ever. Thinking about work without thinking about relationships makes less and less sense in today's rapidly changing milieu. So even if you decide to skip around, we urge you to start with the Chapter Two exercises.

1

Reflections on the Changing Workplace

Dr. Seuss:
". . .You can get so confused
that you'll start in to race
down long wiggled roads at a break-necking pace
and grind on for miles across weirdish wild space,
headed, I fear, toward a most useless place.
The Waiting Place. . ."

WE BELIEVE THAT the biggest changes that have resulted from the pandemic and other events of the last several years affect both the content of our work and the context of our relationships at work and at home. In this chapter, we highlight in abbreviated form some of what we consider to be major changes and trends influencing our work life over that last decade or so.

The list of transformations in the nature of work is long and likely to continue to grow longer as we move further into the 21st century. Debates proliferate as well about these changes, oscillating between the angst associated with job losses and exploitative digital sweatshops as contrasted with the promise of increased flexibility and the shaping of new, more creative jobs. The list of changes—before the Covid-19 pandemic accelerated the rate of change—includes, for example, the development of new forms or organization such as telework and virtual teams; the growth of artificial intelligence, robotics and automation; the proliferation of freelancing and contracting; the remaking of the traditional corporation and the slow demise of the bureaucratic or psychological contract in which employees traded off labor for employment security; and the spread of digital crowdsourcing platforms and open models of production and sourcing of ideas.

3

We've organized these types of changes under three generic headings: *New Ways of Working; New Organizational Realities*; and *Global Turbulence*. Under each of the categories are particular changes that we see as ubiquitous, significant, and consequential. We want you to think about their impact on you specifically.

Some of these changes may have touched you directly and some not. Some of these shifts are a consequence of the two-plus years of the Covid-19 pandemic, and some are the result of longer-term global, societal, organizational, and market changes. Some seem certain, powerful, and likely to alter the career landscape for many, if not all, of us. Others seem less so.

What will last in what we have described in the Preface as a *VUCAA* world is impossible to know. Yet it is well worth considering some of these apparent changes identifiable today as a way of thinking about your career to date and preparing as best you can for an always unknown future.

> **Our first suggestion for you is to reflect on the following twenty changes**

As you reflect on these changes, make some notes for yourself of what the actual *major* changes were for you in your particular situation and just how they affected or influenced you and those close to you. You will later look back at your assessment of these changes and examine the implications they have had for you and your career.

Changes in Work

Upheavals, Adaptations, Permanent Shifts?

New Ways of Working

The "Great Resignation"	The Covid-related "Great Resignation" led scores of employees to quit their current jobs to look for and find positions that offered more attractive work conditions and prospects.
Smaller Teams, Mounting Workloads	Cost cutting and reduction in the labor force increased the responsibilities and workloads of those employees who remain in the organization.
Gig Economy	Part-time, contract, and transient work accelerated during the Covid-19 period and continues to grow partly because workers now expect more control over the location, timing, and conditions of their employment.
Distance Has Eroded Trust	Openness and trust in the workplace often decline when employees work remotely at a significant physical distance from one another.
Here Today, Gone Tomorrow	As the time employees spend in any one organization shrinks, the value of organization-specific knowledge and skills is diminished, if not lost completely.
Fuzzy Job Ladders	Fewer corporate careers are of the "up or out" variety and are increasingly played out as a combination of climbs, lateral moves within or across organizations, periods spent out of the workforce, and even planned or unplanned descents.

| Distance Has Undermined Support | One of the important roles often played by teams and groups in organizations is to provide support for its members (psychological safety). Yet with the widespread adoption of remote work, face-to-face support may wither. |
| Footloose and Fancy Free | Geographic moves made for a variety of reasons—for work, for love, for opportunity and adventure, for affordability, for a healthier environment, for better weather—are increasing for those who can afford it, but this often means loosening the ties we maintain with friends and family who remain in place. |

New Organizational Realities

Job Loss Blues	Many of the jobs that were put on hold or vanished during the height of the pandemic are not coming back since organizations have learned that they can do without such job roles.
Distributed Work, Local Control	As jobs grow more flexible and variable, work schedules and job assignments are increasingly being set by local teams or groups, based on their collective responsibilities and the individual needs of their members.
Never Smart Enough	The fast pace of technological change has turned many of us into perpetual learners, our knowledge constantly requiring upgrades.
Need for Speed	Flatter, team-based, increasingly lean and nimble organizations are on the rise as a means for surviving in a highly competitive and constantly changing marketplace.

Who's the Boss?   Hierarchical authority declines as the competence and understanding of subordinates increases; skilled operators, technicians, frontline workers, and many others often know their jobs better than their supervisors or managers.

Twenty-Four Seven   It is difficult to set and enforce specific on and off hours for virtual work such that employees face job demands that seemingly never let up.

Hyper-Specialization   Jobs are demanding more in terms of skills and knowledge than in the past as the technologies that underlie work are growing more complex.

Global Turbulence

Global Village Competition   Work that could be done remotely—virtual work—allowed for hiring practices that transcended geographic limits and greatly expanded labor markets.

Tomorrow's Factories   As work becomes increasingly digitalized, fewer people occupy operational and production roles, and more people are required in knowledge-based service and support roles.

Forget Loyalty   Rewards for dedication and long service are no longer expected or rewarded in many organizations and are increasingly seen as reducing motivation and violating performance-based incentive systems.

Job Jitters   Worries over a volatile, uncertain economy and possible job losses often result in placing higher expectations on ourselves at work and over-performing, often working overtime, to secure our positions.

And finally . . .

Pandemic Dread   With the World Health Organization's estimated death toll from coronavirus reaching 18 million (and counting), our day-to-day sense of everyday security, safety, and stability has drastically fallen.

Now Consider:

How have you been personally influenced by these changes?

Now Consider:
How have you been personally influenced by these changes?

For example:

I am out of work and have to start all over . . .

I have been working at home and want to continue to do so . . .

I miss the routine of office life . . .

My goals for what work should be have really changed . . .

I have a different relationship with my family and friends now . . .

I now realize that I have to go into a new line of work . . .

So much has happened, I don't know where to begin to cope with all of these changes . . .

Try to list and be specific about particular changes and how they altered your previous assumptions, relationships, and ways of doing things. These reflections will prove helpful later as you consider what aspects or activities of your career to date you wish to keep, let go or evolve, and do differently in the future.

_____

_____

_____

_____

_____

_____

Following Your Reflections, What Actions Can You Take?

Having thought now about how some of the changes that have occurred have affected you in general, we move on in Chapter 2 to provide a framework and a tool to more deeply understand how these changes have or have not affected specifically *your relationships* both at work and at home.

2

Building a Relationship Map

Dr. Seuss:
". . . Somehow you'll escape
all that waiting and staying.
You'll find the bright places
where Boom Bands are playing . . ."

BECAUSE OF PANDEMIC "stay at home" and "lockdowns," how, where, and with whom we work on a daily basis is still changing. Many of us have (a) learned to work from home, (b) have had to interrupt our work for unanticipated durations, (c) have left or lost our pre-pandemic jobs, and/or (d) are considering a new line of work altogether.

These changes in work lives will inevitably affect relationships in our family and with our informal lives with friends and colleagues and the "boom bands" that help us through the tough times.

Many of you will face the following questions

1. **What kind of work will you do?**
2. **Where will you work?**
3. **How much will you work?**
4. **With whom will you work?**
5. **What kind of relationships will you have at work, in your family, and with friends?**

Before you tackle the career aspiration issues in the first three questions, it seems inevitable that some old relationships will have to be reestablished, some new relationships will have to be created, and adaptations will have to be made in the balance of work, family, and personal pursuits. This will be true in how you relate to colleagues, the people above you and below you, and the people with whom you share tasks and objectives, whether in person or in virtual office settings.

We now provide you an opportunity to examine those relationships so as to visualize whether you need to make new choices in how you manage relationships and career directions. When you have gained some insight into your "map" you will then be able to relate those relationships to the new map of work and career options that build on the career anchors exercise.

We suggest you start with mapping *relationships* because we believe that as you look ahead you will be driven more by **multidimensional life-work considerations** that are broader than just career anchors. To this end, the following exercise consists of several parts, which together may take up to an hour or so.

You will draw relationship maps that consist of the various people to whom you are connected. You will then read about different "levels" of connection or relationship and fill those in. You will then reflect on these relationships in order to decide what level you desire in them as you look ahead in this *VUCAA* world.

Another caution—it is tempting to flip ahead and get a sense for where this exercise is going in terms of career issues. You can do that. But, we think, nonetheless, that these exercises are more powerful if you proceed through the steps we have outlined and let the insight unfold as you go. We encourage you to go through this page by page as laid out to maximize the learning.

Building the Basic Relationship Map

In the first exhibit (Exhibit 2.1) below you'll find a blank version of what we call a "relationship map."

A "relationship" exists if you and the other person each have some expectation of how the other person will respond as you are interacting with each other. A relationship is by definition *mutual*. Each of you expects something of the other even if you do not interact with that other person on a regular basis. Each of you has some kind of impact or influence on the other.

Your relationships organize most of the behavior of your daily life, so it is important to see their impact on you and your impact on others.

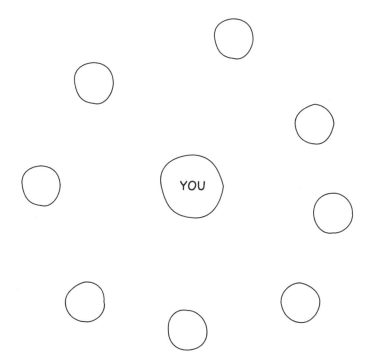

Exhibit 2.1   Relationship Map Initial Template

Step 1: Circles as building blocks

Start with a blank sheet of paper (we would suggest 8 ½ by 11 or A4 to give you ample room to draw your relationship circles). Draw yourself in a circle in the approximate center of the page, and draw any number of blank circles surrounding yourself.

Step 2: Circles for work relationships

The blank circles are used to represent the key people with whom you work. Write their names in the circles that are arranged around you (Exhibit 2.2). Consider leaving plenty

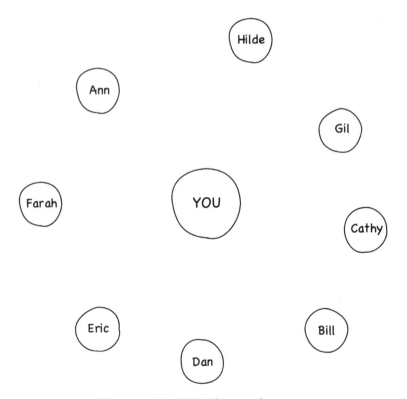

Exhibit 2.2   Filling in Work Relationships

of room to add circles for other key relationships that come to mind as you go through this process.

You can use the location of the circles to signal status or hierarchy by putting the people whom you think of as above you, beside you, or below you in the circles that are in those positions.

Step 3: Circles for family and personal

Draw more circles representing key family and personal relationships that affect your work and personal life (Exhibit 2.3). Children and a partner or spouse can absolutely be included. Any other relatives can be included if they influence your work and personal lives.

The goal is to identify the particular people in your life who have an influence on you, who have expectations of you, and whom you would normally describe as being connected to you, that is, relationships that affect you on a daily basis. **(Feel free to add extra pages or use a larger template [poster size] if you want to widen the map even further.)**

Step 4: Circles for lost or future relationships

You should include in this map not only your current active relationships but also draw circles for relationships that you lost or have become more distant because of the pandemic or for other reasons. Add relationships that you have gained or believe you will gain as you look ahead (Exhibit 2.4).

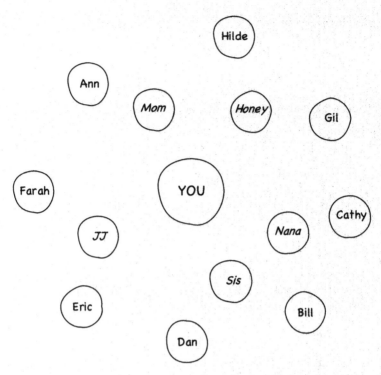

Exhibit 2.3   Filling in Personal Relationships

You may discover that you have many relationships in your life and that these have been affected in various degrees by any number of events of the last decade or two. You have work relationships, family relationships, friendships, and community relationships. For purposes of this exercise put as many of them on your map as needed to help you gain a complete picture of the interpersonal network in which you live, using extra pages if necessary to make the whole picture clear to yourself.

Visualizing as much of the network as possible on this simple hand-drawn map(s) may be critically important in illuminating how external and internal forces have affected all those connections in a variety of ways, with your work relationships most likely feeling the brunt of the impact.

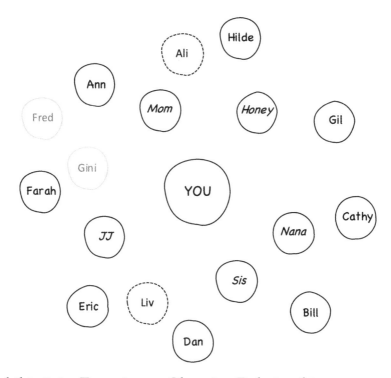

Exhibit 2.4   Emerging or Changing Relationships

Step 5: Drawing lines to identify relationships

You can now draw lines to these various relational circles to express the intensity of the different relationships you have identified (Exhibit 2.5).

Draw heavy solid lines where the relationship is steady and frequent, and draw broken or dotted lines where there is a relationship but it is not as strong, using for now just your intuition of what it means to have a strong, weak, or distant relationship. Next, we will give you some categories for analyzing *levels* of relationships that will enable you to be more precise about the lines you have drawn.

Keep an open mind and take your time to include all the important people with whom you feel you have a relationship.

If you are doing this exercise with someone else, then each of you should do it and compare your maps to see whether either of you have left out some important categories of relationships such as people who are not physically present at work or at home but have an impact on your work and home lives.

One important thing to note—it is tempting to include circles for functions, divisions, or roles that you interact with. As a first step, that is fine. However, the primary intent of this exercise is to focus on the relationships with a particular person.

This exercise is about the people, not the roles. If you have put a placeholder circle for a role (for instance, "legal" or

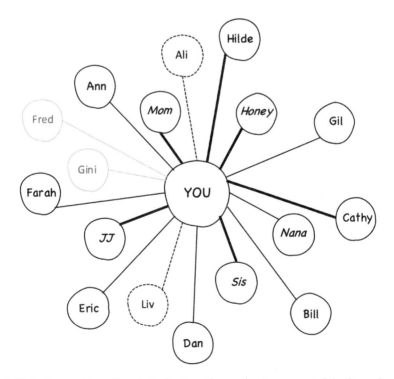

Exhibit 2.5   Depth of Relationships (using variable lines)

"accounts payable" or "HR"), take a moment and identify that person who you spend the most time with or expect to spend the most time with. You are trying to move beyond the simpler notion of role relations and deepen your thinking about the whole person to whole person relationships.

At this point, take some time to reflect and think about what it means to have good or bad relationships and weak or strong relationships. Then familiarize yourself with our model of "Four Levels of Relationship" described in the next section. When you finish, we will ask you to consider: (1) the level of relationship you have with the various people you named, and (2) the level of relationship *you think you should have* with them as you look ahead and consider various kinds of work situations that you may find yourself in.

Four Levels of Relationship

We intuitively sense that we have a very strong relationship with some people or a very weak relationship with others. Some relationships feel good and others not so good. We feel more connected with some people than with others, and we may feel that relationships at work seem quite different than the relationships at home. Similarly, relationships we have with friends are different from those at work and at home, even though there is often an overlap as we think of friends at work and our spouses or partners as our best friends.

Our relationships at home differ according to whether we are talking about our spouse or partner, our children, our parents, our in-laws, or other relations such as cousins and nephews, grandchildren, and so on. Or cultures have trained us in how we are supposed to relate to these various categories but also allow us a great deal of freedom, which results in having better or worse relationships with different relatives.

To make sense of all this so that we can be proactive with our relationships, we need a model or taxonomy. We are not inventing this model, we are applying some labels to *levels* of relationship that are generally recognized in most societies. How each of these levels will play out in the particular culture in which you live will depend, and should depend, on your particular socialization or learning. These levels should not feel limiting any more than a wireframe or foundation only provides the broad outlines into which you fill in the details that fit your particular situation.

> **Level −1: Domination/Coercion through power**
>
> **Level 1: Transactional Relationships based on role behavior**
>
> **Level 2: Personal and "Personized" Relationships**
>
> **Level 3 Emotionally Intimate Relationships**

Level −1: Domination and Coercion: This level is characterized by a dramatic disparity between the side with power and the side with essentially no power. We label these "minus one" because we are describing a relationship, yet it is a *negative* relationship; level zero would imply no relationship. Examples here could include managers in a coercive organization or shop floor bosses in a sweat shop.

We would use *Level minus 1* to describe prisoners, POWs, and even slaves relative to the guards or "masters." There are even times that we dominate friends or acquaintances or members of divergent cultures or ones we consider lower or inferior. There are times we may relate to people much younger and less experienced, or older and less facile, in a domineering way that we would have to admit is *Level minus 1*, domination or coercion.

These relationships are usually less comfortable for the dominated person, but if one is required to remain subordinate, it is sometimes even possible to adapt to and tolerate the lower role. And there is a time dimension— there are relationships that are intended to be *Level minus 1* to begin with, as a tough form of inculcation or indoctrination and which will then use the experience of this disparity of power to strengthen the bonds as the relationships develop. In the armed forces, *Level minus 1* bootcamp may well have the effect of reinforcing stronger bonds later on, as a tough ordeal shared by those who have made it through. The same might be true of tough training and inculcation experiences such as medical school and medical residency.

Step 5A

Now, go back to your relationship map that you drew in Step 5 (Exhibit 2.5) and put a minus 1 (−1) next to any lines that you consider to be Dominating or Coercive.

Level 1: Transactional Relationships based on role behavior: These are common daily relationships that we have in casual conversation with strangers on the street or seatmates on public transportation. These relationships are almost always scripted by the roles we have learned and implicitly agree upon when we go to stores, restaurants, banks, or deal with service people whose help we need, including professional helpers of all sorts (such as a plumber, a mechanic, and even a doctor or lawyer).

We treat each other as fellow humans whom we trust enough to not harm us and with whom we have polite levels of openness in conversation, but we do not feel the need to know each other except in our various roles and statuses. Professional helpers such as doctors and lawyers fall into this category because their role definition requires them to maintain relational decorum or "professional distance."

This level often includes fellow employees, bosses, and direct reports with whom we interact in terms defined by our official roles or ranks. Whether or not we trust them and are open with them depends on the situation—transactional relationships in work groups can be open and collaborative but are more likely to be defined as competitive situations, especially with colleagues, who are ultimately competing with us for the same promotions or other incentives for good performance.

In our various commercial dealings, we typically expect transactional relationships to be zero-sum or "my gain is your loss" and hope to walk away from them with a feeling of having gotten "a good deal." We maintain professional distance and expect ourselves and our counterparts to be equally distant.

These relationships can be felt as good or bad within the tight bounds of a hierarchy, and personal connection is inevitably constrained since we are typically talking about requisite transactions between competitors. We should not hide from the reality that our modern Western capitalist system relies on this basic organizational principle of competing for promotion, for which Level 1 transactional relationships seem perfectly suited.

The most important point to be noted about Level 1 role-based transactional relationships is that they can lend themselves to exploitation and destructive competitive behavior.

Step 5B

Now, again go back to your relationship map (Step 5, Exhibit 2.5) and identify and label all of the Level 1 relationships.

Level 2: Personal and "Personized" Relationships: These relationships reflect that we see the whole person, above and beyond their role or status, such as in our friendships. We can describe these connections as personal but not necessarily intimate.

Such relationships may begin at a transactional level but evolve through mutual curiosity and interest into deeper relationships by way of *"personization."* This is a process of mutually connecting with each other as whole people, suspending concerns about role and status, by asking each other more personal questions and revealing more of ourselves to the other person.

This kind of relationship implies a deeper level of trust and openness in terms of (1) making and honoring commitments and promises to each other, (2) agreeing to not harm each other or undermine what we have agreed to do, and (3) agreeing not to lie to each other or withhold information relevant to our various tasks and obligations.

Step 5C

You may not have thought of this as applying to the work situation, yet you can identify on your map those links that are clearly more collaborative, more open, and more trusting. Mark them as Level 2 on your relationship map.

Level 3: Emotionally Intimate Relationships: These are relationships where stronger positive emotions and intimate contact may be involved. As such, these connections are often considered taboo in organizations and work settings. Trust here goes beyond Level 2 in that the participants not only agree not to harm each other but assume that they will actively support each other, with particular bias, whenever possible or when needed. The openness between two people at Level 3 develops to the point of sync or telepathy that much of the other's reactions and state of mind can be anticipated. Simply put, Level 3 means you can finish each other's sentences.

A form of Level 3 relationships can evolve in groups and teams when the work is highly interdependent and every outcome, every step of the way, is mission critical. Such degrees of high expectation of success (possibly even life or death) require that these teams or groups spend disproportionate amounts of time together (as in every waking hour).

A kind of "professional intimacy" may develop in work situations that we would describe as Level 3, or perhaps more accurately Level 2.5. Examples here can include high-performance teams in the military (e.g. Special Forces such as Navy SEALs), in professional sports teams, or start-ups that exert their drive to succeed in the 2x normal work week commitments expected of key employees and founders. In these high commitment and highly interactive contexts, *Level 2.5* is a likely and hopefully positive by-product of the time spent together.

Step 5D

Now, lastly, return to your relationship maps and fill in those links that have reached this level by putting a 3 (or 2.5) next to them.

Assigning levels to each relationship is done by progressively adding numbers to the map. If your relationship map is complete with all lines—intense as well as distant or broken—and marked appropriately, your map may look something like the representation in Exhibit 2.6.

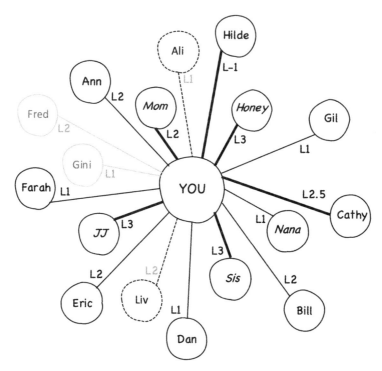

Exhibit 2.6   Mapping Levels of Relationship

Gaining Insight into Your Relationships

The purpose of doing this is to gain some insight into how your various relationships differ in level because we believe that the pandemic, perhaps even the last decade as a whole, has had an impact on work and home relationships and can be captured visually by mapping relationship changes over time.

You should feel free to create multiple maps if you prefer to differentiate social categories of relationship such as just work relationships, just family relationships, and any other categories that you feel will be important in how you plan your future. If you have drawn your map on new sheets of paper, add pages and plan to keep these notes for future reference.

You may also wish to elaborate this exercise by also showing where you think a relationship has changed from the past to the present by using numbers and arrows between them for each line to depict past, present, and desired future relationships.

In Exhibit 2.7, our hypothetical subject, the "you" in the exhibits, has updated her map to capture the change from the departure of some colleagues in her work life and the new relationships that should now feature prominently on her map.

Also note that she has updated her relationship with Hilde, her boss. This is a visualization of her intent, or the result of her making a conscious effort, to draw closer to an otherwise

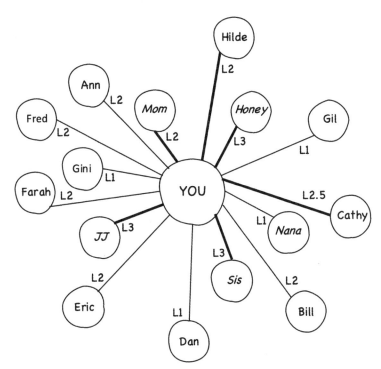

Exhibit 2.7   Changing Relationships and Levels

domineering manager and forge a deeper bond based on mutual openness and building mutual trust.

We recommend that you do this exercise carefully at first and be ready to redo the map or maps frequently—the visualization can really help sort out complex relationship dynamics in your life-work balance. We hope relationship maps will prove to be an important guide not only for the here and now but also as you think your way into the future and want to come back to these maps from time to time as you process new experiences. Visualizing the present and gauging future progress are both helpful outcomes of this exercise.

Why All This Relationship Stuff?

We have taken you through a multifaceted exercise on the nature and levels of relationships because we believe that it is relationships that have changed and evolved most in the last decade. We also believe that those relationship changes have had a major impact on what we work on, where we work, with whom we work, and how "personized" our work will be as we look ahead.

Perhaps the most important question pertaining to future work is whether we want to work closely with people and develop *personized* relationships at work or are we satisfied with the professionally distant relationships that so much of our office work has become and/or that working from home engenders.

How does the quality of relationships have a direct impact on communication and, thereby, on the quality of our work?

We hear about the importance of psychological safety, learning to speak up, more transparency and openness, and the need for more employee engagement in the workplace. All of this implies significant cultural changes in the relationship dimensions of how work gets done in the age of *VUCAA*.

This exercise is essential if you are to accurately assess your own work needs and anchors, as well as the kinds of organizations you will consider joining. What demands will you make on your supervisors and managers, what kind of culture will they have grown into, and what will their demands be of you?

If you are already or will be a manager, what will you expect of your direct reports and what will they expect of you? If you are to report to a general manager, what do you expect of him or her? We have encountered numerous examples in the next generation of employees expecting to be related to at Level 2, as whole human beings, and finding themselves in professionally distant Level 1 or sometimes even in Level −1 work relationships. It is commonly found that people leave jobs primarily because of a bad boss, and we think that this feeling is most likely the result of being treated transactionally (Level 1) as just a role instead of being seen as a whole person (Level 2).

In summary, you need to be honest with yourself about what you expect in your work, what you will settle for, and how you will know what is going on in your place of work. We believe your various relationship maps will help you do that.

3

The Changing Nature of the External and Internal Career

Dr. Seuss:
". . . Oh, the places you'll go!
There is fun to be done!
There are points to be scored.
There are games to be won."

OVER THE PAST decade and particularly during the height of the Covid-19 pandemic, the career concept has undergone a subtle shift. VUCAA has made the notion of a "standard" career increasingly slippery and ambiguous. To think of the career as, say, a lifelong set of formal and more or less predictable steps through job movements and/ or promotions to a final stage leading to retirement from the workforce is gradually going out of fashion as *impermanence* characterizes the occupational landscape. Better to think of occupational and organizational careers as a set of jobs undertaken over time within a given context.

The "External" Career

A career from this broad perspective is what you put on your résumé (or sometimes leave out). It is a formal recounting of your occupational history in terms of the jobs you have held and places you have worked. This more or less objective representation of your work history we call the "external" career to distinguish it from the subjective representation of the career in terms of how we feel about our work over time, how our work becomes attached (or not) to our sense of self or personal identity, and how it organizes our thinking about our occupation.

Examples of external careers include those of tradespeople, who go through formal apprenticeships and licensing; those of physicians, who must complete medical school, internship, residency, rotating through different areas of specialization, eventually moving into a particular practice; or those of general managers, who must go through several business functions, have experience supervising people, rotate through the international division, serve on the corporate staff before being given a generalist job as a division general manager.

In a similar manner, we can talk of career paths that define the necessary or at least the desirable steps to take along the way to some goal job. Clear instances of this kind of explicit and formal path are found in the military and the civil service with their well-defined ranks, clear rules for how one advances from one rank to another, and the salaries associated with each level.

These are all representations of external careers and say little or nothing at all about how individuals define their career to themselves—what the career means to the person who travels that path. This is the subjective side of careers, the "internal" career.

The "Internal" Career

How internal careers develop is a lengthy and experiential process that depends on real-world encounters with the work world and the lessons one takes away from such encounters. With each job change or promotion we learn something of what we are good at, what motivates us, and what we value.

This process leads most of us to develop a set of career preferences—from the rudimentary or inchoate in our early work years to a more fully formed set of preferences that come with accumulated experience. These preferences organize our occupational choices and give us a sense of a reasonably coherent internal career even if we hop from job to job, organization to organization, or even from occupation to occupation.

With each educational or job experience, we have an opportunity to learn. It is important that we go beyond just judging each experience as good or bad, fun or not, useful or not and to ask, "What have I learned about myself?" As we grow, we need to learn not only what is "out there" in the arena of work but also what our own reactions are to the experiences. These reactions are best thought of in terms of three specific domains:

1. *Skills and competencies.* You need to learn from each experience what you are good at; that learning comes both from your own assessment and from the feedback you receive from others.

2. *Motives.* You need to learn from each experience what it is you really desire; early in life we think we know what we want, what our career aspirations are, but with each experience we discover that there are things we like or don't like, that some of our aspirations are unrealistic, and that we develop new ambitions.

3. *Values.* You need to learn from each experience what it is you value in the context of what your occupation or organization considers important, what your colleagues value, and how the kinds of organizational cultures you encounter fit with those values.

As we gain experience, we become more familiar with each of these domains until an emergent self-concept forms composed of what we are good at and not good at, what we want and do not want, and what we value or do not value. This self-concept builds on whatever insight we have acquired from the experiences of youth, education, and career experience to date. It remains an emergent self-concept until we have had enough real occupational experience to get to know ourselves in each of these domains.

Such learning may require many years of actual work experience. If you have had many varied experiences and have received meaningful feedback with each one, clarity in your self-concept will have developed more quickly. But if you have had only a few jobs in the early years of your career or have obtained minimal feedback, you may still be unclear about your competencies, motives, and values.

Your talents, motives, and values may become so intertwined that it may be hard to separate them out. We become better at those things we value and are motivated to do, and we learn to value and become motivated by those things we happen to do well. We also gradually learn to avoid those things that we do not do well, although, without clear feedback, we may cling to illusions about ourselves that set us up for repeated failures. Motivation without talent will eventually fade, just as talent without motivation will gradually atrophy. Conversely, new challenges can reveal latent or hidden talents and introduce a motivation that we simply had not had an opportunity to experience earlier.

Journey toward Self-Discovery—Career Anchors

As you accumulate work experience, you have the opportunity to make choices; from these choices you begin to ascertain what you really find important. Dominant themes and values emerge that influence your orientation toward life. You may have had a vague sense of these elements earlier but in the absence of actual life experience, you do not know how important they are or how any given talent, motive, or value relates in a subjective hierarchy to other elements of your total personality. Only when you are confronted with difficult choices do you begin to discover and decide what is really important to you.

Clarification and insight provide a basis for making rational and empowered work and career decisions. The self-concept you are forming begins to function more and more as a guidance system that constrains career choices. You begin to have a sense of what is "you" and what is "not you." This knowledge keeps you on course or in a safe harbor. As people recount their career choices, they increasingly refer to "being pulled back" to things they have strayed from or, looking ahead, "figuring out what they really want to do" or "finding themselves."

This process leads people to gradually move from having broad goals to a sense of knowing better what it is that they would not give up if forced to make a choice. Career anchors, as defined here, are the elements in a person's self-concept that he or she will not give up, even in the face of difficult choices. If work does not permit expression of those anchors, people will find ways of expressing them in their hobbies, in second jobs, or in leisure activities. Work, for some, is just "doing a fair day's work for a fair day's pay" and seen as simply fate, beyond our control. This is especially true in the more machine-like or automated industries of the past and continues today in certain production functions though less so in what has been dubbed "knowledge work."

Today, however, we are less likely to settle for the mysterious workings of fate and wish to exercise more control over our careers. The learning process associated with the forming of such career leanings or anchors is increasingly regarded as self-determined and has been of necessity speeded up by the pandemic and many other changes, as highlighted in Chapter 1. Let's face it: VUCAA has destabilized not only our external careers but our internal careers as well.

We can still think of anchors as stabilizers, but the winds of the pandemic and rapid social and technological change have pushed us into many different directions. These changes in our occupational and organization worlds have led us to new ways of looking at career anchors.

The same patterns of competencies, motives, and values still operate within us as we move through various jobs, but our ability to match these internal anchors with given jobs or organizations has become much less stable and more problematic in recent times. Many occupations and jobs today can be identified with several anchors to a greater degree than in the past which raises the possibility of partially satisfying several of the career anchors rather than looking for "the *one* thing we would not give up."

Many of us have found that our career—like a financial portfolio—can become a portfolio of different jobs reflecting different competencies, motives, and values. Some jobs will match well with what we identify as our primary anchors, what we would not give up if forced to make a choice, but we always knew that other anchors were also operating in us. We can now see more clearly that different jobs and even different occupations can satisfy some of the secondary or tertiary anchors that we identify in ourselves.

We can also begin to see that the different anchors overlap and can be thought of as derivative from the prime anchor or anchors. And we can sense that the anchors we associate with our work lives have become entangled much more than we realized with our relationships—to the point that the quality of our work, family, and social relationships have become the primary basis for both our economic and personal well-being.

It is for the above reason that we began this book with analyzing our relationships before we present the eight career anchors. The basic anchor categories have not changed over time, but their importance to the internal career has evolved. Given that evolution, we now invite you to explore some of the elements of your internal career.

4

The Eight Career Anchor Categories

Dr. Seuss:
"I'm afraid that *some* times
You'll play lonely games too.
Games you can't win
'cause you'll play against you . . ."

INVERTING DR. SEUSS' caution, you *can* win this game because *one of you is going to win.* And winning means getting a better sense of who you are. From the original research in the 1970s to now, this has been the common thread—understand your anchors to understand your career trajectory.

One very important point is that the anchors do not correspond precisely to particular occupations because in most occupations, such as business, medicine, or the trades, it is possible to be in that occupation with different anchors. For example, in any sample of doctors, lawyers, or even police officers you will find successful occupants with different anchors because in these occupations it is possible to pursue that line of work for different reasons. When you look at the descriptions and examples, think about your competencies, motives, and values in general terms, not necessarily in terms of what you are doing right now in your present work.

To familiarize yourself with the eight anchor categories, read the descriptive paragraphs and the example stories associated with each of them. For each anchor think of the description relative to yourself: Is it "Totally me," "Sort of like me," "Not so much me," or "Definitely not me." After the description, we provide two hypothetical examples, not real people, simply prototypical examples to illuminate the anchors.

45

TECHNICAL FUNCTIONAL (TF)

A "Totally me" on this category means that you want to get better and better in your area of competence and would prefer your work to remain in that area of competence. What you consider to be your particular skills and areas of knowledge are a product of your talents, education, and work experience. You are proud of them, and it gives you an identity as being the best in some area of specialization.

That work area can be anything from being an expert technical sales rep, an engineer, or a teacher. Or it can be in a craft such as electrical, mechanical, or construction. You are good at it and you value it, and if a promotion or new offer took you out of that area of work, you might resist the move, especially if it brought you into a role in which you could no longer practice your area of competence.

TF Examples

Ted Friedman got his BA in political science but had a great interest in teaching. He went on to get his teaching credentials and specialized in teaching social studies in high school. After a few years, he discovered he was very good at it, enjoyed it very much, and resisted any move to other fields or into administration if it removed him from high school teaching. He attended advanced training courses in how to become an even better teacher and took on some jobs coaching younger teachers.

Tania Field graduated with a BS degree in computer science and then went on to business school and emerged with an interest in computer engineering. She then took various jobs in large companies that permitted her to develop her interest and competence in this area. In two of these companies she was promoted to supervisory jobs but found out she did not like the management side of this work and left for a smaller start-up where she could concentrate on developing her own specialized skill set.

AUTONOMY (AU)

A "Totally me" for this anchor reflects your strong need to do things on your own, free of the constraints and rules that characterize most organizations and work projects. What you really want to hold on to is a work situation or job context that gives you the feeling of freedom and independence you need. At the extreme you might wish to be self-employed, but many traditional organizational jobs such as teaching, consulting, research and development, and even sales can also allow a great deal of freedom.

If you are in an organization, you will want to remain in jobs that allow you flexibility regarding what you work on and especially when, where, and how you do your job. You sometimes will turn down opportunities for promotion or advancement to a bigger project in order to retain your autonomy.

AU Examples

Alice Updike started her career after graduate school as an independent management consultant and was so successful that in a few years she had to hire several others to help her handle all of the business. As her company grew, she realized that she did not like managing the organization. What she liked was the consulting and the freedom that it provided. As a result, she sold her company and went back to being a freelance consultant.

Arthur Unger started his career in the human resources department of a large corporation and quickly discovered that he neither liked nor respected many of the rules and rituals of that organization. He tried developing a more autonomous research role, but found that life in a large organization was just too intrusive. He left the organization, went back to school, received an advanced degree in psychology, and began teaching and developing his own research projects at a midsized liberal arts college. He was successful, and over the years, he moved on to several larger universities able always to pursue his evolving but independent research interests.

CHALLENGE AND RISK (C&R)

A "Totally me" in this category means that work for you has to be perpetually challenging. You thrive on tackling the seemingly unsolvable problems, to winning out over tough opponents, or on overcoming difficult obstacles. For you, the most important reason for pursuing a job or career is that it continues to provide challenges, that it permits you to win out over the seemingly impossible or vanquishing the toughest competitors.

Some people find such pure challenge in intellectual kinds of work, such as the engineer who is only interested in impossibly difficult designs; some find the challenge in complex group situations to get people to work together;

some find it in interpersonal competition, such as the professional athlete or the salesperson who defines every sale as either a win or a loss. Capital markets positions, such as investment banking, trading, venture capital, and private equity, may also provide the level of irresistible risk associated with this anchor. Novelty, variety, and difficult puzzles become ends in themselves, and if something is easy, it becomes immediately boring.

C&R Examples

Charlie Riordan joined the US Navy because he wanted adventure. He was able to join the aviation wing and became a pilot flying off aircraft carriers. He spent all of his discretionary time honing his flying skills so that if at some future time he had to confront an enemy in single aircraft-to-aircraft combat, he would prove to be the superior pilot. He kept himself fit and ready at all times, waiting for the opportunity to prove his own superiority. In sports and in games, he was extremely competitive and could never stand to lose. When his flying days were over, he reluctantly took a desk job but continued to be a fierce competitor in all of his non-job-related activities and loved solving difficult puzzles.

Christina Richmond graduated from business school with a major in finance and took a job on Wall Street as a bond trader. She enjoyed the intrinsic intellectual and inter-personal challenge that this job provided. When offered an opportunity to be promoted into managing a group, she refused because she wanted the stimulus of one-to-one competition with others and the challenge of solving problems under conditions of uncertainty and incomplete information. She found sales relationships intrinsically exciting and defined every situation as a "combat" in which either she or "the other" would win. She was able to remain in this kind of competitive environment throughout her career.

ENTREPRENEURIAL CREATIVITY (EC)

A "Totally me" in this category reflects your need to create an organization or enterprise of your own, built on your own creative abilities and your own willingness to take risks and to overcome obstacles. You want to prove to the world that you can create an enterprise that is the result of your own effort. You want your enterprise to be financially successful as proof of your abilities. You measure yourself by the size of the enterprise and its success.

You may be working for others in an organization while you are learning and assessing future opportunities, but you will go out on your own as soon as you feel you can manage it. This need is so strong that you will tolerate many failures throughout your career in the search for that ultimate success. You may also find that once an enterprise is successful you may want to move on to try to build yet another enterprise.

EC Examples

Ellen Cohn started out as a part-time real estate agent in her local area while raising her children. During this time, she also started several "spouses financial clubs," focusing on successful investing and also built up a small retail jewelry business. After her children were older, she established her own successful real estate office. Over the next several years, she built a chain of real estate offices in her region and ended up running a sizable real estate empire.

Ed Corbin started his engineering career in Boston, but he was always on the lookout for opportunities to start something of his own. He developed some skills in the area of finance and discovered that certain financial procedures that were very successful in one industry were totally lacking in another industry. He moved to Denver, where he saw the opportunity to create a consulting company that would sell this new financial tool and built up a multi-million-dollar business. He also wanted to open some retail fish stores that sold ocean fish in this "mountain area," but this business failed for lack of a market. In time, he sold the financial business and invested in some mining interests and eventually retired from being a business entrepreneur to become a dean in a new business school in the area that he viewed as another type of entrepreneurial venture. He called himself a "serial entrepreneur."

GENERAL MANAGEMENT (GM)

A "Totally me" in this category means that you have a desire to manage broadly and pull together the various elements of an organization or project. What you desire is the opportunity to climb to a level high enough in an organization to enable you to direct the efforts of others across functions and to be responsible for the output of a particular unit of the organization. You want to be responsible and accountable for total results, and you identify your own work with the success of the organization for which you work.

If you are presently in a technical or functional area, you view that as a necessary learning experience and may even accept a high-level management job in that function. However, your ambition is to get to a generalist job as soon as possible. You want to be able to attribute the success of your organization or project to your own managerial capabilities based on analytical skills, interpersonal and group skills, and the emotional capacity to deal with high levels of responsibility and the difficult decisions that inevitably come with those levels.

GM Examples

George Madison graduated from business school and entered a program in the communications industry for "high potential" managers. This program involved annual rotations through the various business functions. Eventually, George was given a chance to supervise a group and discovered that he liked working in that role and was good at it. He realized at that point that he wanted to climb the managerial ladder and became quite impatient with the slow rotational program. After looking for possible career opportunities elsewhere, he took a managerial job in a smaller but rapidly growing firm, quickly moved up the promotional ladder, and was shortly running a company sooner than would have been possible at the communications company. He successfully ran and grew this company for twenty years before retiring from that job.

Grace Morgan started in a large computer company as a computer programmer. After five years in various programming jobs, she took over a technical group, displayed some talent in managing the group, and discovered that she really liked the managerial side of her job. Over the next several years, she took over larger and larger groups, learning during that time a lot about operations, finance, and marketing. When a company in a similar line of business needed a new CEO, she was recruited by a headhunter for this job, took it, and has successfully run this company for the last ten years of her active general management career.

SERVICE, DEDICATION TO A CAUSE (SV)

A "Totally me" in this category means that you want your occupation and your daily work to mean something of significance to you, that you want to pursue work that achieves something of value, such as making the world a better place to live, solving the environmental problems of how to adapt to global warming, improving harmony and cooperation among people, helping others, improving workplace safety, curing diseases through new products, and so on.

You would pursue such opportunities to perform socially meaningful work even if it meant changing organizations, moving to a new location, or receiving lower pay. But you would not accept transfers or promotions that would take you out of work that fulfills values that to you are significant and worthwhile.

SV Examples

After college, Stella Vargas took a position in the human resources department of a large corporation that had the reputation of caring for its people. What she wanted was an influential position in the organization where she could influence corporate human relations policies. She knew, however, that the career system in the company would move her through other functions first and strongly resisted efforts to move her into those other functions. Over time, she convinced her bosses to implement some new HR policies based on her humanistic values. As her influence grew, other organizations noticed her work, which led eventually to her being recruited to become head of organization development for a Fortune 100 company.

Stanley Vance majored in biology and forestry during his college and graduate school years. He became a research professor at a state university and was able to work on his concerns for how corporate policies were endangering the environment. A major aluminum company recruited Stanley and asked him to develop and implement mining policies that were environmentally responsible. Stanley spent ten productive years implementing his ideas in the firm, but when a new corporate administration wanted to reward him by promoting him to a general management position that was not in the environmental area he decided to return to teaching and environmental research.

STABILITY AND SECURITY (S&S)

A "Totally me" in this category means that you really value and need stability and security. In your decisions to accept a job or a kind of work you seek employment security or tenure in that job or organization. This need can show up in concern for employment stability, financial security such as medical benefits, pension and retirement plans, or geographic stability in the sense of being in an area where you feel you can always find a secure job.

Such stability may involve trading your loyalty and willingness to do whatever the employer wants from you for some promise of job tenure. You are less concerned with the content of your work and the rank you achieve in the organization, although you may achieve a high level in line with your talents. Everyone has these needs to some degree and they can become paramount at certain life stages, but if you strongly identified with this category, it means that this is *always* a concern for you.

S&S Examples

Stan Seward grew up in a small town in which his father had a small business. After college, Stan worked in two or three companies that moved him around the country in various functions. He felt he learned a lot from his willingness to take on the variety of tasks assigned to him, never turning an assignment down. But when he was ready to settle down and raise a family, he returned to his hometown and decided happily to enter the family business because it would provide a secure career and geographic stability.

Sally Smithson grew up in a family that could barely afford to send her to college. But they managed to do so, and she chose engineering as her major because it would guarantee that after four years she would be able to go directly into a job without graduate training. After graduation, she went to work for a large electronics firm and developed a set of skills that she knew were on demand and would be required indefinitely. She was content with the working conditions, good benefits, and generous retirement plan offered by the organization, often accepting assignments that were not particularly challenging but that she was glad to do because it made her feel needed and hence more secure in that organization.

LIFE-WORK INTEGRATION (LW)

A "Totally me" reaction here reflects your desire to balance the demands of work, family, and taking care of yourself. You may have a relationship with a significant other who also has a career so that the two patterns of work have to accommodate to each other. You want to make all of the major elements of your life combine together toward an integrated whole, and you therefore need to develop a work situation that provides enough flexibility to achieve such integration.

You may have to sacrifice some aspects of your career—for example, a geographical move that would be a promotion but would require your significant other to give up his or her career aspirations or would require your children to leave a good school or would require you to relinquish commitments you have to your community. You feel that your identity is more tied up with how you live your total life, where you settle, how you deal with your family situation, and how you develop yourself rather than with any particular job or organization.

LW Examples

Lisa Walden, in mid-career on a general manager track, had to choose between taking a very large promotion to the headquarters of a company located in a rural area of the Midwest and a much less prestigious job in a corporation located in a large urban area on the eastern seaboard. Her husband was in a highly specialized technical field, and his chances of finding a job in the urban area were much better than in the rural region. Lisa chose the less prestigious job in order to maximize both of their chances to have satisfactory careers.

Lou Woods was a middle manager working in a European subsidiary of a large oil company with its headquarters in New York. He was on a general management track in the US organization, but he had a German wife, who was attached closely to her German family and culture. When their son was eight years old, Lou was offered a major promotion in the US company that would require leaving Germany and moving to and remaining in New York for at least the next five years. Lou turned down the promotion and opted instead for a lesser job in the subsidiary because he and his wife decided that they wanted to bring up their son in Germany where they felt most comfortable.

Career Anchors, Modernized

The eight anchor categories that you have just reviewed cover most of the types of career that we found in the research on men and women in recent decades. There is every reason to believe, however, that the pandemic and the recent changes we have described earlier in the book may produce other kinds of work self-images that are either derivatives of the eight categories or brand-new variants.

What this means is that you may not have found a single category that is *truly YOU*. Instead, you may have found that you are a complex combination of many features, or that you have experienced change in yourself or your circumstances over the last few years such that you are feeling less and less "anchored" and that you are now, more than ever, "at sea" searching for a "steady course" or a "safe harbor."

The earlier research clearly showed that many of the anchors remain stable when we followed people further into their careers; but here, as well, we are seeing changes in how people are viewing themselves as a result of the new social and technological environments we are facing. In today's world, several anchors can serve as your internal guides, and they may function together across many different kinds of occupations or jobs or even in your leisure and hobby activities.

Some examples of contemporary careers—akin to our brief illustrations of the eight career anchors above—are described below. These three cases, unlike the previous idealized examples, reflect a mix of anchor leanings that shift with changing circumstances and life stages. As with all of our case examples in this book, these are stories of composite individuals, with entirely fictional names and representative though not actual details.

Katy Dean, Single, 12 Years of Work Experience

Katy Dean was working as a nurse at Kansas City Metropolitan Hospital when the pandemic hit. She called it the most frightening time that she could remember in 10 years of nursing. Not only was she worried about catching the virus during her shifts, but some of the patients took out their anger and frustration on her. "I was working double shifts, making lots of money, but it was exhausting." She enjoyed taking care of people but reached a point where, she said, the burnout was real. She had to get out of that job.

She left to pursue a long-standing dream: To become a farmer. She had been growing fruits and vegetables in her backyard for years. But she had to learn how to run her own farming business, so she signed up for a class taught by *FarmShare* Kansas. She subleased a small piece of land to grow fruits and vegetables on a larger scale and now sells her produce at local farmers' markets. She says of her new line of work that she still wants to nurture people but in a different way. It's very satisfying for her to grow nourishing food for people.

Farming is much less predictable than nursing, and the financial insecurity worries her. Still, she says she is much happier now, works on her own schedule, is outdoors much of the time, is not physically and emotionally drained at the end of the day, and wakes up every morning energized about what she is doing.

> *This case illustrates a different blend of anchors including Service, Autonomy, and, through both nursing and farming, Technical Functional competence. There is seemingly a slight preference for the Service anchor but clearly there is a mix of anchors that at various times ebb and flow in salience.*

Caroline Gonzales, Married, One Child, 14 Years of Work Experience

Caroline Gonzales grew up and went to college in the Boston area. After graduating, she started out working part-time in a variety of jobs: as a hair stylist at several salons and as a hostess for a few high-end Boston restaurants. Then, she and her sister opened a small wine store, The Vin Bin, on Boston's Northshore and successfully ran it for 10 years. Unfortunately, when sales began to fall in 2018, they had to close the shop, and Caroline started working full time as a server in a restaurant where she had previously worked— until the pandemic.

She was unemployed for a brief time and happy to return to the restaurant when it reopened in June 2020 for limited hours. But she needed more work. She had a friend who was doing online sales of health and wellness products and learned the company she worked for was looking for help. She had a little knowledge about the business but, through her friend, got a part-time position.

Even with the addition of sales work, she had time for something else, what she calls her "little side hustles." When she heard about a part-time opening for a position in a well-regarded charity organization in Boston, she jumped on it. Moreover, she was familiar with the organization—she'd volunteered there during her Vin Bin days reviewing grant applications—so she applied. She got the job and today is in the position of a part-time community outreach manager.

Balancing shifts at the restaurant, the sales job at the wellness products firm, and the position with the charitable organization requires some juggling. But she enjoys the mix—especially the chance to make a difference in the community through her outreach job. It's a zig-zag career to be sure, but she appreciates how each job seems to fit into what she calls her "pockets of the day."

> *This case has Caroline joining a workforce of millions—freelancers, gig workers, contract workers—who string together various endeavors into full-time work. While there does not seem to be a dominant anchor, her story suggests that in various times and jobs, the anchors of Autonomy, Service, Entrepreneurial, and most recently, General Management are present.*

Jamal Rodgers, Married, Two Children, 23 Years of Work Experience

Jamal Rodgers joined the Seattle Police Department in 1998 after having served in the Marine Corps for six years after high school. Going to school part time, Jamal earned an associate degree in criminal justice from a local community college while in the department. He was a patrol officer and loved his job. He had no desire to climb the ranks to sergeant or lieutenant despite being encouraged by senior officers to do so, nor, for that matter, did he want a more specialized, investigative position in the detective division.

As a patrolman, he occasionally served on the crisis intervention squads and spent three years on one of the SWAT teams in Seattle. He enjoyed the security of a civil service career and the generous retirement benefits that kicked in when he eventually "pulled the pin" and retired after 20 years with the department.

Jamal has been for some time an enthusiast of outdoor sports—everything from mountain biking, rock climbing, trail running to whitewater rafting. The more arduous and competitive the activity, the better it suited him. Less than a year after he retired, Jamal took a position as a wilderness guide for an established local company that offers strenuous backpacking adventures in the Cascade ranges, along the Olympic Peninsula, and as far north as Alaska.

It is a company he knew well as a former client and had developed several lasting friendships with a few of the company's guides. He started work about a year before the pandemic put on hold some of the tours he had hoped to lead, but he's optimistic that the business will soon bounce back. It's certainly not as steady as a police career but far more flexible and venturesome, taking him to many places he had always wanted to experience and explore.

This case is perhaps typical of mid-life changes in occupation and the shifting priorities about the kind of things we want to do. The mix of anchors support one another even though they may seem somewhat contradictory. The initial period was marked by the Stability and Security anchor backed by the Challenge and Risk and Technical Functional anchors. This is followed by shifting the anchors' order of importance in the later career movement, toward more Autonomy and Life-Work Integration but still pursuing Challenge and Risk.

Moving On . . .

In the chapters to follow, we do not ask you our original anchor question of "What would you not give up, if you had to make a choice?" Instead, the next two chapters will provide you with more opportunities to figure yourself out in terms of your anchor preferences across all eight anchors. Do not assume that you can easily define a singular anchor as dominant. It is important, therefore, to remind yourself that the goal of this entire exercise is **for you to figure out what motivates you, what your values are, and what you are really good at. You may find that none of the anchors fit you very well and that you will have to find your own words to characterize who you really are at this stage in your life.**

To anticipate the next step, the best way to do this deeper dive into who you are is to first review your own *work history*—what jobs you took, when you took them, why you took them, and what you learned from each job move. You can do this by yourself, or you can do this with a partner and have that person discuss this with you based around the "interview" questions we provide you in the next chapter.

5

The Career Interview

Dr. Seuss:
"All Alone?
Whether you like it or not,
Alone will be something
You'll be quite a lot."

WE CAN ALMOST hear Dr. Seuss saying, "Except when you are not." The career interview, whether conducted with a friend or partner or with yourself and a recording device, helps you to move beyond that feeling of being alone. It helps to be heard, as you describe your job history.

As noted, the best way to get useful insights into your own career anchor issues is to review that work history before you take the online survey. This chapter will lead you through a formal way of collecting this information about yourself.

Learning from Your Career Story

This interview is an important exercise in developing a personal narrative, an individual story, of your career to date. It may take a few hours, and those who have done this exercise invariably report *learning a lot* about themselves as a result.

While it is not required that you do this with another person, it can be very useful to explain your journey, to make your story clear, to a friend or partner. As you go through the questions below, your partner can play the active role of interviewer. Alternatively, the partner can be the active listener to you, reinforcing your explanation of the career

67

journey by following along and interjecting questions for clarification.

The purpose of this interview phase is to understand the through-line, to highlight when and where you opted one way or another. A partner can help you in this process, with one caveat—the partner cannot be the one shaping the story. The greatest risk is that the partner's interpretation becomes your story. Any partner in this process should be helping you recall and not coaching you on what it means.

If it is not possible to go through this process with another person, consider simulating this dialogue process with a computer or smart phone. One approach that we favor is using the dictation and transcription features on a current PC, Mac, or IOS or Android device. Using a "Voice Note," or "record and transcribe" app, your device can act as a partner, "listening" and transcribing what you say. In our experience, this will force you to be more complete, honest, and open about your career journey. Simply thinking about it will not force you to articulate it. So transcribe and, in any case, take notes and make connections to your sense of which anchors resonated and resonate with you.

The transcription is the reward for carefully articulating your story and will in turn reengage you with your journey. Is the transcription correct? Did I leave anything out? Does seeing it written out in this way help me see any patterns?

Whether with a partner interviewing or an app transcribing, your goal is to gain insight, perhaps even clarity, on where you have been with your career. You may also see patterns that suggest future directions. Still, the primary goal of

this "interview" phase is to fully capture the past, before you get ahead of yourself into the future.

Questions for the "Interview"

Education

Did you go to college (two year or four year)?

If not, did you seek alternative training after high school?

If you went to college, how and why did you select it?

What did you major and minor in? Why?

Did you go to graduate school? Where and why?

What was your concentration in graduate school? Why?

First Job

What was your first "real" job after college or post-secondary school training?

Did you have long-range goals at that time that this job helped establish?

Was your first job a *net positive* or *net negative* in your early career journey, and why?

Were there any strongly memorable lessons you could take out of your first job experience?

The Next Job

When and why did you make your first job or career change?

Did you leave a job (or bad boss) or did you seek something different?

How did this move work out?

Did this move help clarify career aspirations? How, or why not?

And Then What?

When and why did the next job change happen?

Were there any other life events that played a role in the job change?

Review Each Job Change until the Present

Turning points or transitions? Look at the long arc (or recent arc depending on your career stage).

Did you experience any major turning points?

Do you perceive these moments differently now than you did then?

Can you describe career high points so far? Low points?

Do you think your career aspirations or goals have changed in response to these highs or low?

Has your vision for an ideal career changed?

Do you have a final career goal or ultimate job you are working toward?

Perceptions of You at Work

In describing yourself to others, personally or in interviews, how do you characterize your strengths and passions?

Can you easily articulate your major competencies? What are they?

Do you have what could be described as "core values" that guide your work decisions?

How do you think others might describe your career arc? Would they get it right?

What patterns do you see that would clarify any misconceptions of your career arc?

As you reviewed your job history did any of your leanings and preferences really stand out, and would the anchors help you understand these preferences? Did you evolve any of your thoughts about which anchors seemed to fit you most and least? What turning points came up in the job history? Lastly, were there any surprises for you as you reviewed your job history?

6

Career Anchors Assessment

A Preview of the Online Experience

Dr. Seuss:
"On and on you will hike
And I know you'll hike far
And face up to your problems
Whatever they are."

IT IS OUR hope that you will work through the Career Anchors assessment and realize the opportunities to leverage your strengths and move beyond what you feel are "problems" in your career trajectory.

The online assessment, https://www.careeranchorsonline. com, that accompanies this book offers an easy way for you to test your insights about yourself with a set of questions derived from the original longitudinal *Career Anchors* study.

We have ordered the self-insight exercises so far—reflection, relationship mapping, the partner/personal interview, and now the assessment so that you have multiple perspectives on your career journey.

The first part of the online assessment consists of 32 questions for which you score your reaction, whether in alignment or disagreement with the sentiment expressed in the statement.

Examples of the kinds of statements that you will score are as follows:

- *I have always felt most successful and accomplished when I could use my specialized training/expertise in my work.*

- *I am always on the lookout for ideas that motivate me to start my own business.*
- *Being a general manager is more attractive to me than being an expert in a particular technical domain.*

You will gauge your agreement with the sentiment along the following scale:

"I feel this way or agree with this sentiment . . ."

0	Never
1	Seldom
2	Often
3	Always

There are 32 items in this format. It takes about 10–15 minutes to go through and react to all of the items. You may start to see a pattern in the kinds of statements, but do not let that distract you. The idea is to react to each of the items individually, and then let the online system put them together into your pattern.

Your pattern will represent preferences or leanings in your career choices around the eight anchors that we have described. Rather than simply rank-ordering these preferences, we provide a graphical representation of your preferences for the anchors. The graphical representation is in a "spiderweb," or "radar" chart format.

The numbers that will appear on the vertical scale of the emergent anchors chart are simply the result of arithmetic to measure relative importance of each anchor. Keep in mind that it is the pattern of the lines that matters, not the numerical scores per se.

To help you interpret your own career "spiderweb," we provide the following example from one of our career journeys described in the previous chapter.

Recall Jamal, who worked for the Seattle Police Department. What insights would Jamal gain from taking the 32-item Career Anchors assessment?

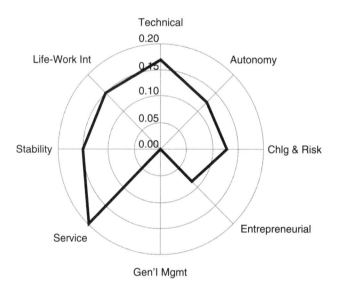

Exhibit 6.1   Jamal's Career Anchors

Jamal's Career Anchors pattern suggests a number of things about his work preferences: He puts a high priority on Service, he values his Technical-Functional base, and has little interest in General Management. Jamal shows a balanced strong interest in Stability and Life-Work Integration, which may reflect the fact that Jamal has been through career transitions and has found that he needs to honor his family's needs in his career journey. Seeking Security in his career is part of this realization. Jamal does have a leaning toward Challenge and Risk, particularly of the physical sort—recall that he joined a SWAT team and has pursued outdoor guide challenges in his later career. Perhaps most interesting in this is that Jamal is showing a leaning toward Autonomy that may not have been as prominent when he was a police officer working for a large city PD. It is certainly possible to lean toward Autonomy and Service simultaneously.

The Career Anchors charts array the eight anchors across from each other, but these should not be thought of as polarities per se. Any pattern, any blending of career preferences is possible. The career anchors items are designed to explore your preferences from different angles, different phrasings that will trigger different reactions. One way or the other, your impression of your Career Anchors chart will likely be one of surprise, delight, confirmation, and possibly disappointment. Regardless, it should be taken in the spirit of learning. Whether Jamal agrees with his "spiderweb" or not, he will learn something from it.

Your Own Career Anchors Profile

It's now time to create your own baseline career anchors preferences. So go online and create your own spiderweb. On visual inspection, does this align with your expectations? Are you surprised? If you did the interview with a partner or solo, were you expecting to see preferences clustered where they were, or were you thinking your preferences would present a different picture? And if you did the interview with another person, we would urge you to have a discussion with the same person who interviewed you about your Career Anchors chart. Does it fit the interviewer's sense of your career preferences?

You should hold on to the chart for reference when you are thinking about the pros and cons of your current position and what really matters to you. When you are asked to describe yourself, your strengths, and weaknesses, the visual should be both memorable and helpful.

7

What's Next? Growth Intentions

Dr. Seuss:
"You'll get mixed up, of course,
As you already know.
You'll get mixed up
With many strange birds as you go.
So be sure when you step.
Step with care and great tact
And remember that Life's
A great Balancing Act."

ONE OF THE reactions that is common after going through the career anchors process is surprise, which then triggers seeming contradictions. Part of you feels one way, and the career anchors results may lean another way.

We may all feel like entrepreneurs or CEOs, but when we go through the mapping, interview, and assessment, it gets more complicated, more nuanced. Generally speaking, by looking at relationship maps, interview transcripts, and the online assessment you may do a better job of capturing where you were and where you might want to be as you look ahead.

The next and final step in an assessment of your career is to get a sense of how you would like your career to develop and what you might do to bring it about. To this end, the *growth survey* should provide you with ideas about how your own work and life situation could unfold as you look ahead.

Your Own Growth Profile

When you registered with the online system, you should have received an invitation that directs you to another phase of assessment:

This part of the career assessment is structured similarly around the 32 items that you reacted to in the last chapter, from not very important to very important. But, this time, these items are focused on growth with the statements phrased as career growth objectives:

"To realize my career aspirations, I think I need to improve…"

Examples of the kinds of growth statements you will respond to are:

- I need to become better at figuring out how things work and how to fix things myself.
- I need to be more willing to integrate both the challenges of work and family.
- I need to continuously develop my specialized knowledge and skills.

Similar to the Career Anchors assessment as outlined in Chapter 6, you will react to these statements on this 0–3 scale, but here the assessment is gauging the relative importance of the growth objective. If the growth intention is not important at all, you would score it "0," "1," and so on, according to this four-point scale:

0	**Not Important**
1	**A little**
2	**A lot**
3	**Critically Important**

Once you have gone through the 32 career growth or skills development items, a now familiar "spiderweb" will provide you with a visual perspective on what is important to you and what is not. These growth items are organized around the same eight anchor categories so you can compare your anchor assessment with your growth intentions or aspirations.

This would be a good time to take the Growth Intentions assessment. You will get the now familiar spiderweb chart overlaid on your career anchors preferences chart. For interpretive purposes, it helps to have an example as a guide.

Returning to our career example Jamal Rodgers, we can see that his growth intentions (the dotted line) departs in some ways from his anchors (the solid line). Our interpretation of the anchors and growth intentions follows below (Exhibit 7.1).

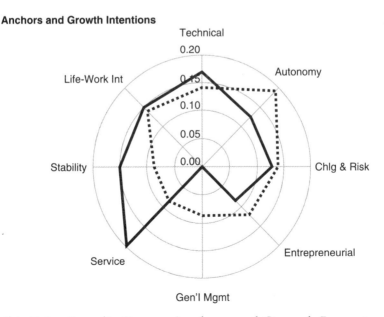

Exhibit 7.1   Jamal's Career Anchors and Growth Intentions

Looking at the dotted line representing the growth intentions, we can see a theme emerging that Jamal feels the need to develop Entrepreneurial skills, become more comfortable in Autonomous work situations, and develop some General Management competency. He does not feel any need to work on Service as the beginning of his career was entirely devoted to public service. This is not to say that Service is no longer important to Jamal. Rather, the growth intentions (dotted line) suggests where Jamal believes he needs to grow for the next phase in his career journey.

8

Five Career Anchors Stories

Dr. Seuss:
"And will you succeed?
Yes! You will, indeed!
(98 and ¼ percent guaranteed)"

IN ORDER TO help you interpret your Anchors and Growth Intentions charts, and to illustrate possible connections between the two, we will now describe in some detail five cases that we have recently encountered that highlight various changes, connections, and combinations of work, home, family, and friendship issues. These cases illustrate not only how each person saw their own career anchors but, importantly, how they saw their own growth or developmental needs—the areas they felt they needed to improve upon.

You might make some notes to yourself in each case where you see similar things happening in your situation and then compare your notes with some of the brief observations we have made about how these cases illustrate new connections and combinations that are more and more common in the changing conditions of life and work.

In all, the two sets of 32 items and the graphical representations are an easy way for you to see your career journey and where you would like to take it or where you would like to grow. And, as we've suggested above, hold on to your Career Anchors and Growth Intentions chart for reference when you are thinking about or planning your next move. When you are asked to describe yourself and your goals, these visuals could be as useful as broad self-description or a possible informal elevator pitch when job hunting (or hopping).

Are these five career journeys success stories? Absolutely, in the sense that vital insights have been gained through all of the ups and downs. Kate, David, Sarah, Carlos, and Maia are all fictional seekers based closely on actual cases that were recounted to us. Please note, however, that the specifics—the people, locations, organizations—mentioned in each case are disguised.

These are very relatable stories, and least surprisingly, they are all deeply affected by the Covid-19 pandemic. As we are writing in summer 2022 in the US, Covid is on another upswing and impacts to work and life are still profound. Covid-19 will have a long tail, with its impacts reaching out in all likelihood for another 5 to 10 years as part of our new normal. For our five stories here, the impacts of the pandemic are fresh. However, the pandemic is only one driver in these career journeys, as you will see.

Kate

This is Kate Mazeroski's story. Kate has a BA in economics, is single, and at this point in her journey she had six years of post-college experience.

> After I got my degree from a small liberal arts college on the east coast, having done well in economics, I was able to secure a first job with a large, well-known financial consulting firm. I got lucky and was relocated to San Jose, CA, near where I grew up. My assignment was to work on compliance for large banks, usually at client sites, so I travelled a fair amount in that first year or two.

Even so, the job was not only boring, it was somewhat upsetting—I did not really click with my boss, and the hierarchy felt oppressive, with what seemed like more emphasis on long billable hours than on rational client service.

This was an important early learning experience for me. The lessons I was apparently supposed to take away were not only to follow the boss's orders and, more seriously, not to question the way the whole project was organized. Even though the project I was on was to help the institution improve, it felt like we were primarily driving up billable hours with uncertain returns for the client. This was too much for me to accept, and I shortly thereafter looked for opportunities to leave. With the help of an independent recruiter, I was able to move directly into my next opportunity.

The next job I took was with a California-based start-up. It was exciting to be part of a small team, I really liked the two founders, the spirit of entrepreneurship was fun. Until it wasn't—the mission turned out to be a little off what the market needed, the CEO left, and the company was eventually folded into another entity.

For me, as a sales and market development manager, the writing was on the wall, and I left when I secured a much more attractive opportunity. At that age and in that market, I did find a fair amount of opportunity and interest, working with sales-oriented recruiters who were very encouraging. The good news was I had pivoted from the big firm, got into the start-up game in sales and marketing, and I could start to pick and choose.

This is when I felt I could take the chance with balancing my work interests with my personal interests, I guess you could call it "self-actualization." I had wanted to move to a smaller city with recreation built into the lifestyle. This was made possible by the emerging category of all virtual jobs. I found a great opportunity at a company based on the East Coast, with an immediate manager in the Pacific Northwest, and the ultimate freedom to live wherever I wanted provided I could get a fast network connection for videoconferencing. For me, it was Boulder, CO, and it could have been many places similar.

The job I took that allowed me to move to Boulder was with BleekerSW, a company headquartered in New York. When Covid hit, it created all sorts of changes, including the company becoming an entirely remote work organization. This suits me very well since I came to Boulder for the lifestyle it allowed, especially for the freedom to work on my own time schedule. I've now got a (rental) house, a dog, and the frequent opportunity to dive into outdoor activities in all four seasons.

The specific job I have is part of a seven-person sales team. Of the seven, I've met only two people face-to-face although I get along with everyone on the team. In contrast to some of my previous jobs, I really like my boss. She originally hired me while she was living in California but has since moved to Georgia. The work I do is typical of sales with various individual and team performance targets. I've gotten useful feedback from my boss, and the team seems to operate smoothly. And I'm doing well. Soon, I'll have two people reporting to me—a step up in the organization.

I should note that BleekerSW has a great wellness program that is free to all employees. We can access free coaching programs that take up various development and wellness issues with coaching provided by licensed psychologists and coaches. The company provides the program to all ~200 employees who can access whatever the announced program of sessions or exercises that are offered on any given week. A surprising number of employees take advantage of this as a way of dealing with the variety of challenges that arose during the pandemic. It is certainly the most supportive organization I've ever worked for, and I feel fortunate to be associated with such a forward-thinking team.

What I've been able to do in Boulder is to follow my values and put together a work and life situation that maximizes my freedom and autonomy. The only thing I miss is more in-person contact among the employees. As I said, at the moment, I've met only a few members of my team in person. Naturally, we talk frequently about getting together someday when Covid wanes. Yet, in spite of the absence of everyday face-to-face contact, we still feel that we know each other pretty well.

Will I play out the rest of my career at BleekerSW? Not likely, I guess, as a graduate program is probably in my future. For now, I'm quite satisfied and no longer do I look around for something better. I'm happy here and find the work and organization amenable, a good fit for me. I do know, however, that if BleekerSW doesn't work out, I'd seek out another remote job, it's a great way to work.

Career Anchors and Growth Intentions Assessment

Kate's Career Anchors and Growth Intentions chart is shown below (Exhibit 8.1). As you will see from the chart, there are certain themes that came out in her story that

Anchors and Growth Intentions

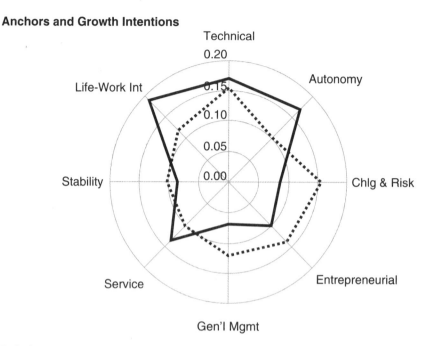

Exhibit 8.1   Career Anchors and Growth Chart for "Kate"

clearly show up in the chart. In particular, the line extending toward Autonomy is not surprising: Kate chose to work autonomously and remotely when she moved to Boulder and began working for "BleekerSW." Similarly, the high value of Life-Work Integration is as expected; Kate was quite intentional in realizing this personal value. A subtler theme for Kate is her interest in being Technical-Functionally strong at what she does and also notable, her leaning toward Serving other people in her work.

Shifting gears and looking at the dotted line, the growth intentions, we can see a theme emerging that Kate feels the need to grow her General Management and Entrepreneurial skills, in addition to increasing her ability to handle more Challenge and Risk as she grows in her career. She does not seem to feel the need to increase her Stability nor her value for Serving other people as these are either less important or already being served by her existing career direction. Lastly, it is notable how her intentions to grow her skills again emphasized Technical Functional skills. For Kate at this stage of her career, it is easy to see from this chart that a graduate school or professional program in which she could increase technical skills and receive some formal general management training might well be a very positive step for Kate to consider.

David

This is David Lewis's story. David has a BA in finance, is married with two children, and at this point in his journey he had 15 years of post-college experience.

Like a lot of people, I started baking bread in the early days of the pandemic. It was a way of filling my time and was in fact something I enjoyed. I got pretty good at it and started giving some of what I was baking out to relatives, neighbors, and friends. They all said they loved what I was making. It's crazy, I know, but as a consequence, I decided to get out of finance for good and take up something completely different from what I had done before. What was basically a new hobby became a new career.

In July of 2019, I got laid off from my finance job; the result of a Wall Street merger and the redundancies that took place afterward. I'd been in finance ever since graduating from college about 15 years ago. I had done pretty well, working for three rather prominent firms, gaining more reach and responsibility in my job and, not surprising, I was making very good money. I probably could have landed another decent job right away—in fact, I had a couple of tempting offers to join other firms—but I decided to kick back and, as they say, spend some time with the family.

In my old job as director of research with an investment firm, I was of necessity up and out the door before my kids even woke up. By the time I got home at night, they were asleep. I figured the layoff gave me the excuse to step back and take some time off and figure out what I really want to do. I really needed to see my kids more as well! Looking back at all my jobs in finance, I was fairly miserable but just kept on pushing. Each job was overworking me. I was dead-tired almost all the time and usually coming into the office even if I felt sick. But I stayed because that's what you were supposed to do if you had a desirable position in the industry and wanted to advance. I wanted also to be the best provider for the family even though I hardly ever saw them. When I left the company, I planned on eventually returning to finance, just not right away, maybe in a year or two with the right firm. But events and the pandemic conspired to change these plans.

By February of 2020, at the beginning of the Covid crisis, I was home and baking every day for a couple of hours in the afternoon—occasionally my wife and our two daughters helped out when their routines allowed. They would waltz in and out of the kitchen doing some of the prep work and clean up. Slowly, however, baking began to take up more and more of my time as I was now capable of producing multiple batches of rather delicious—if I do say so myself—sourdough bread and assorted pastries. I continued to share the results of my work with those around us. But the idea was gradually growing on me that maybe, just maybe, I could do this full time. Baking became rather quickly a much more significant pursuit, more than just a hobby.

We live in a coastal suburb not far from New York City. We moved outside the city about six or seven years ago when our daughters were quite young, and we've become more and more active in town affairs over the years. My wife, for example, teaches math in the local public high school and got to know many of the parents of her students. She loves her job, the kids, the people she works with, and, unlike me in my former jobs, has a reasonable work schedule. During the height of the pandemic of course she was teaching from home on videoconferencing. Quite an adjustment, but she seemed to handle it with aplomb.

Our daughters are in a private day school a couple of towns away. They also video'd-in to school during the first Covid surge. We're members of a local beach club that provides lots of family activities during the summer months, activities that were rather unhappily restricted for a time. In the past, I served for a couple of years on the town's Advisory and Finance Board, so I also know a lot of people in the town.

All in all, it's been a comfortable, if somewhat stereotyped, suburban lifestyle. The pandemic has disrupted some of this lifestyle, but we've managed to get through it for the most part without too much distress. The children found a way to contract Covid, but thankfully it turned out to be a mild, almost asymptomatic form. We are now all vaxed, boosted, and healthy. Luckily, no one in our immediate family or close circle of friends has died or come down with a serious case.

This reminds me that when I was in my old position, I asked for a bereavement leave to go to my uncle's funeral. This was a couple of years ago. The funeral was in Chicago and was to be something of a reunion for family members increasingly spread across the country. I had what I thought was a respectful conversation with my boss but was told in the end this was not the time to take a leave, even a short one. He said essentially, "Tsk, tsk." I guess it's the price we pay for the money we earn. But it got me to thinking: Do I really want to spend the rest of my life letting somebody else's work demands take precedence over everything that was important in my life? I got a chance to do something about it during the pandemic.

So, to get back to what's happening now, I eventually decided that rather than return to the city and to another finance job, I would train myself to become a better and more serious baker. I read and watched everything I could about baking. I volunteered for about 10 hours a week in one local bakery as a jack-of-all-trades and did anything and everything that helped them out—from customer service, to cleaning up, to baking preparation, to actual baking. Because the labor scarcity surrounding this kind of work, it soon turned into a part-time job, and I learned a great deal as a result. I was further able to hone my skills later as a part-time baker at another local shop. These experiences provided real hands-on training, a kind of apprenticeship. I spent about a year doing these odd and varied jobs while continuing to bake at home when I could.

This eventually led to what I'm doing right now. In January of 2022, I started my own baking business, Sandpiper Bakery. I make my bread at the Founder Space, a food and business incubator located close by in a neighboring town. There I make and sell about three-to four-hundred baked goods each week and on weekends at farmer's markets nearby. In about a year or so from now, I'll open my own bakery in the area. I never thought I'd be an entrepreneur, but I guess you just never know. I have no plans to ever again work in finance. It was a grind, and for a time, it was probably worth it. It certainly allowed me the time and space and, importantly, the money to take up baking. But, in hindsight, I should have left finance sooner. It was really wearing me down. But, at any rate, what I'm doing now feels much better, it's the right thing for me. And the kids are no longer waking up and going to sleep in my absence.

Career Anchors and Growth Intentions Assessment

The Anchors and Growth chart for David (Exhibit 8.2) shows a lot of gaps between the lines. This is another way of visualizing that David is making a dramatic career shift. His Career Anchors line represents his life in finance—his priorities were Technical skill in investment research and taking on the Challenges of a Wall Street career, comprising the risk inherent in placing bets in capital markets, as well as the risks associated with climbing the ladder in Wall Street firms. The strong General Management extension in the Anchors line is no less surprising since taking on leadership in the research department meant that David needed to develop his managerial skills as much as his research skills. The Stability extension is also not surprising in that the choice to have stable employment in order to best provide for his family was one of his goals. The contrast is to Autonomy and Life-Work Integration. Wall Street was not offering steady and lucrative employment to allow David

Anchors and Growth Intentions

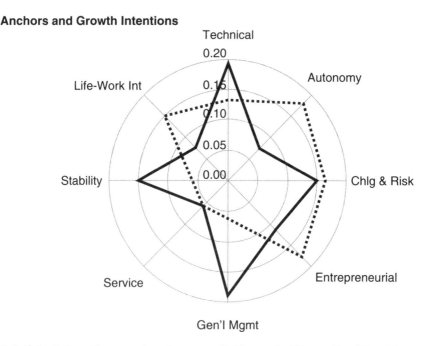

Exhibit 8.2   Career Anchors and Growth Chart for David

to seek autonomy and optimize for time with his family. This was the trade-off David the "banker" made over the past 15 years.

Similarly, the Growth Intentions line fits the "baker" part of the story. David's intentions are clearly to become more comfortable with Autonomy and Entrepreneurship; these are perhaps the two most striking gaps. The shift in values around Stability and Life-Work Integration are also of note and consistent with David's story. He's focused on spending more time with his family while he recognizes the greater risks in sacrificing his Stability in order to make this career pivot from banker to baker.

Sarah

This is Sarah Smith's story. Sarah has an MA in public policy, is married with two children, and at this point in her journey she had 10 years of post-master's experience.

After grad school, I worked for eight years in NYC for a firm called Tech Solutions. It was essentially an IT consulting firm helping mostly big global firms install, maintain, and use tech infrastructure. It was a good job at first but gradually grew into a real grind.

It had a very traditional office life. We were tied to the midtown office, a nine-hour day, 8:30–5:30, but half of the time we weren't busy enough to justify the hours. Nonetheless, we were expected to be in the office every day. But if a client wanted some information or help during your off-hours, you were expected to be available. Chats at 3 a.m. with, say, a Saudi client were not unusual. You were monitored constantly, and idle was the state you didn't want to be caught in.

When the pandemic hit in March of 2020, Tech Solutions shut down its office, gave up the lease, and all business were handled remotely. The company began losing clients by the basketful. I worked in that environment for about a year, and while the job was better now than when we had to be in the office—I didn't have the horrendous commute, going from our place in Brooklyn, to Charlie's daycare in lower Manhattan, to the office—it was still focused on job monitoring and work routines that seemed frivolous.

Then, in January of 2021, they had a mass layoff that I was caught up in. About half to two-thirds of the 300 or so employees in the company were let go. I was the finance director at the time, seven months pregnant and about to begin a four-month maternity leave. Can you imagine a company that fires people who are pregnant and just short of going on a maternity leave?

At the time, I had been interviewing with several companies for a new job. I still liked the tech industry and the kind of work I had been doing. The interview and hiring process in one firm, Graphic Enterprises, based in San Francisco, was pretty far along at the point the layoffs hit at Tech Solutions. And, to my good fortune, they hired me right away. I was out of work for about 24 hours. Not only did they hire me at an increase in salary of about 20–25%, but they agreed to continue my planned maternity leave and even extended it by several months and agreed to my coming back at 60% time. Now I'm working 80% time, and I'll soon go to 100%. My husband Alexander, then a public interest lawyer in NYC with about 10 years of experience, was also working remotely at the time I moved over to Graphic Enterprises. Our baby, Michael, was born in February 2021.

Still living in Brooklyn, we went to visit family in California in May and, surprisingly, didn't return to Brooklyn. The visit was to be a short stay—about a week—yet turned out to be more or less permanent. We soon found a house to rent and had most of our belongings shipped out. We didn't want to come back when the pandemic was running rampant in NYC, and California then seemed to be doing so much better. We were able to stay in California partly because Graphic

Enterprises was totally virtual. We were able to rent out our tiny Brooklyn apartment for roughly what we pay in rent for a four-bedroom suburban home with a large yard. Alexander recently got called back to the NY office as the worst of the Covid-19 crisis seemed to be lifting. But we're now settled in California, and Alexander resigned to become a house husband for the near future—happily I must say.

Anyway, I love my new job. The company was established in January of 2020. It builds coding infrastructure and is doing quite well. It just got Series D funding. It started with 20 people. When I joined, it was up to 60 employees. Now it has about 200 employees. It's a global firm, which means we recruit wherever the talent is found. We can get the best engineers, the best tech people.

Because we work virtually and are not restricted to a particular search area, we have employees in NYC, San Francisco, Nigeria, Singapore, Paris, Barcelona, Italy, all over the world as well as across the US. One thing I like about this firm and the remote or virtual way of doing business is that you get to know a very diverse set of fellow employees. Not the old, boring, same culture sort of colleagues that all live in the same general locale.

I should mention that I think the company tries very hard to be transparent; everything is online, and they seem to be really trying to live up to their values as put out in the company descriptions of processes and ways of evaluating your work. They don't just write their values on the wall and walk away. They help you set work and personal boundaries, and you really can say no to requests others make of you.

There are travel budgets in place to meet coworkers in other cities or countries that are generous—although I haven't been using them, because of Covid. There are twice yearly meetings in San Francisco, where the company maintains a brick-and-mortar office. I love that I have no two-hour subway commute each day. I can choose the hours I work and take vacations and breaks when I want to.

Work is organized around my personal life. If I want to take Charlie or Michael to the park at 2 o'clock, I can do so. Nobody is checking on me. I'm trusted to get the work done. It's a place that respects its employees. Occasionally, say, a couple of times a month, I get away from the distractions at home and go to a local shared-office place and pay for the time I spend there at a quiet desk. Overall, I think I'm far more productive working this way than before, either in the office or at home with Tech Solutions.

I don't really miss the social aspects of the office life. I'm slowly getting to know people at Graphic Enterprises, but it's not the same as seeing them every day, face-to-face. I guess there are questions about what is a work friend. What does it mean? It's not clear to me. There is another colleague at the company who I've worked with together a bit. She lives close by, and we've talked about getting together sometime for dinner but have yet to do so.

The company does encourage visiting coworkers in other cities, where you'd get a tour and learn about their personal lives. But social life is largely restricted to remote daily and weekly meetings with some virtual time dedicated to socializing akin to happy hours where you are not supposed to talk about work or the company.

How long I'll stay here remains to be seen. But, so far, it's pleasant. The company seems to care about its people, and the work is interesting and challenging at times. We are growing, and there are opportunities to increase my responsibilities and expand my job. The transition to this job and to California certainly happened very quickly, seemingly almost spontaneously, clearly brought on by the pandemic and a desire to get away from my previous job.

Career Anchors and Growth Intentions Assessment

Anchors and Growth Intentions chart for Sarah is presented below (Exhibit 8.3). In Sarah's case, her Career Anchors line clearly shows her need for Autonomy and Life-Work

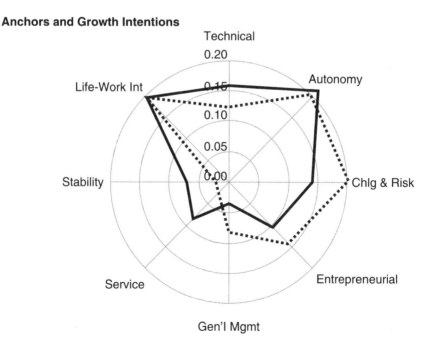

Anchors and Growth Intentions

Exhibit 8.3   Career Anchors and Growth Chart for Sarah

Integration. She has been through some disappointments and keeps coming back to the things she values, balancing life and work and maintaining her independence to work on her own terms.

When we evaluate Sarah's growth line, a couple themes emerge. First, she has a clear "appetite" for taking on start-up challenge and risk. This may reflect the fact that she has been through the disappointment of her first company going downhill and recognizes that in the tech sector, Stability and Security are illusory while tolerating more Risk and taking on more Challenge are typically rewarded. It is notable, however, that she is not trading off Life-Work Integration for Challenge and Risk. She wants to have both. There are companies that are "wired that way," and she seems to have found one in Graphic Enterprises. It will be interesting if the company decides to bring key employees like Sarah back to the office as the Covid threat declines and pare back on the virtual work policy. Sarah may welcome that social immersion, but she does not seem to relish commuting and foregoing Autonomy for the strictures of in-office life.

Carlos

This is Carlos Diaz's story. Carlos has a BA in sociology, is single, and at this point in his journey he had five years of post-college experience.

> The summer of 2020 was really a stressful time in my life. I just spent three years working for Upward Bound, a Boston-based

nonprofit devoted to helping first-generation, low-income high school students make the transition into college. I started with them part time in my junior year of college and went full time after I graduated. I enjoyed the students, and I could certainly identify with them. They came from the same place I did. It was a great job, and in many ways, it was perfect really for me when I was a student. But, frankly, after college it wasn't taking me anywhere, and I was beginning to feel trapped by the mission, which never let up.

This became especially obvious when we shifted to an all virtual way of providing service in response to the pandemic. My bedroom became my office. It was isolating. I was in my room all day looking at the computer. It was monotonous really, spending the day on video with the students. And the job became even worse as I saw the negative effect distance learning had on my students. The seniors that I primarily worked with were forced to forego those high school milestones, little ones like dances, assemblies, football games, to big ones like proms and graduation ceremonies. They became increasingly disengaged with school, and I had to put more and more effort into my job just to keep them on track.

I also had plenty of time to think about what I was doing. It was basically a job with little opportunity to grow, and even though I felt I was doing something helpful and worthwhile, I knew I would have to leave eventually if I wanted a job with more opportunity and learning potential. I started looking around. I really didn't want to go to grad school since I had no clear idea of what I wanted to do. But with a little help from my friends, one in particular, I stumbled into a field that looks as though it will work for me.

In May, as the school year was coming to a close, I gave notice to the people at Upward Bound that I was leaving. And I applied and was accepted to what is essentially a kind of trade school in computer technology, Resolute Coders. The school offered a five-month intensive program in coding. It was costly—but I had a good friend who went through the program and landed a pretty good job afterward in the tech world, so I thought the school would be worth it. He talked it up with me, and it seemed at the time like it was the right thing to do. It would open up jobs for me that were beyond the terminal or dead-end sort. I certainly didn't have any computer skills beyond the rudimentary word processing and internet-search sort, yet I was more than willing to learn. But, wouldn't you know it, fate interceded because just after I heard back from the admissions office at the school that I was accepted, I got some really bad news—all the people in my family, my mother, father, and brother, all came down with Covid. And I got it too.

In early June, I left my job at Upward Bound and became the go-to person for the family. My father was hospitalized, put on a ventilator, and, for a couple of months, we didn't know whether he'd live or die. My mother was pretty sick too but didn't require hospitalization. My younger brother, who was just starting high school, was sick as well but with a much milder form. And like my brother, I too had a mild form.

It was an incredibly stressful couple of months, and I didn't do anything but care for the family. I was buying the groceries, keeping the house up, and even acting as the family policemen by not allowing friends to come to the house. Most painfully for me was the fact that I couldn't even hug my little nieces, who were two and five at the time. Life pretty much stopped. In the end, my father pulled through but has some lingering effects but is now back to work at the USPS. My mother is fully recovered.

As the family got back on their feet, I started the remote classes at Resolute. It was tough, and I found the remote learning, like the high school students I counseled, a bit intimidating. It was super intense, to say the least. I had a lot to learn, and I must say it didn't come easy at first. I wanted to quit a number of times. I was very frustrated.

But about three months into the program as I began to focus more and more on coding—even in my spare time—things began to click for me. I remember working on my portfolio website in my room when I began to think, *Wow, I can really do this.* It was getting easier. It was as if I discovered I had an interesting and exciting power at my fingertips.

I finished the program around November and got lucky. We were required to do a final project for the program, which we then had to publicly explain and demonstrate to the faculty. It was a sophisticated form of show and tell. The faculty also invited outsiders from the tech industry who were curious about what we were doing and just might be interested in recruiting graduates of the program. It was all done remotely, and each graduate had about a half hour to present their work.

For my project, I made a prototype app to help those navigating the immigration system. About a week later, I got several calls from different companies to come and sit for an interview. I was pretty excited, and after a round of interviews, I got a couple of offers right off the bat. My most attractive one came from the Anderson Institute, a science-driven organization just outside Boston that does biomedical research to improve human health. It's a pretty famous place, and I was pleased and somewhat astonished that they hired me.

I started work as an assistant software engineer in January. It's a challenging job but tremendously satisfying. The tech area is a world I never thought of before, but I'm really enjoying my work. And I'm learning so much—about cloud computing, big data collection and storage, information security, and on and on. I think I'm getting fairly good at my job and can see a lot of opportunities for advancement at the Institute and even other places beyond the Institute.

Maybe I was pushed by the pandemic to make a career change sooner than I might have otherwise—although, truth be told, I was burnt out and exhausted with my college advisor role when I started the program at Resolute. At any rate, I couldn't be happier and pleased I made the switch when I did even though it was in the middle of terrible times.

Career Anchors and Growth Intentions Assessment

The Career Anchors and Growth Intentions charts for Carlos is presented below in Exhibit 8.4. In Carlos's case, the years of experience and number of jobs is limited. This can mean that the Career Anchors line is very discrete, representing less experience with career trade-offs than a mid-career job seeker. The other key factor with Carlos is the impact of Covid-19—his life was clearly disrupted during the pandemic and the close calls Covid-19 represented for his immediate family. While we would not expect this to have a primary impact on his career trajectory, we know for most of us, the pandemic had a profound impact on our state of mind. For Carlos, this apparently meant a willingness to try something new and to leave a position that was not fulfilling. Given how quickly the term "Great Resignation" caught on, we can surmise that many of our friends' and colleagues' sense of purpose and preciousness of family and health were deeply altered by Covid-19.

Carlos was in a Service career at Upward Bound. However, he felt the need to change his career course. We can see his motivation to learn a new set of skills and develop some expertise by the strong extension toward Technical-Functional in the Career Anchors and the Growth Intentions chart. Also notable for Carlos is his recognition that in addition to building his Technical-Functional skills, he recognizes the need to take on more risky assignments,

Anchors and Growth Intentions

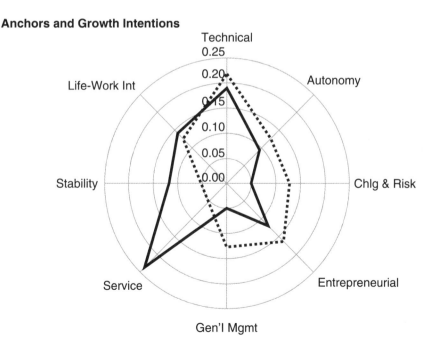

Exhibit 8.4 Career Anchors and Growth Chart for Carlos

build General Management skills, and possibly pursue Entrepreneurial aspirations, which shows strong leanings in both assessments. Carlos's case is a good example of where the chart seems to show a profound shift from Service to Technical-Functional and Entrepreneurial. The question for Carlos will be what his career anchors and growth intentions look like after another five years or so working in software development, a high-growth and very crowded competitive field? Will he see another shift?

Maia

This is Maia Potter's story. Maia has an MS in marine biology, is single, and at this point in her journey she had five years of post-master's experience.

> I had a bunch of so-so jobs prior to going back to school for my master's degree. After getting a BA in fine arts and environmental studies, I worked for a small art education company in Los Angeles where I did day-to-day support activities for the founder. I also worked for several art galleries in LA. All were part-time jobs, none very exciting. So I made a decision then to return to school in an environmentally friendly field, marine biology.

> After grad school at a university in Boston, I took a job in January of 2018 as a program manager at the University's brand-new Global Sustainability Institute. I was one of four program managers. The Institute had been in existence for only eight months when I arrived.

> I worked there for almost two years. In the beginning, I enjoyed the job and felt I was contributing to the overall goals of the

Institute, which I supported wholeheartedly. Traditional work hours were required, nine to five. We were dependent on grants—from government agencies and various foundations—for our funding, and the pressure was always on to keep the money coming in. I co-wrote proposals and was responsible for compiling a database capturing the work of hundreds of researchers.

Those I interacted with as part of my job were my boss, Jane, various student interns, and a host of researchers from other universities or independent marine biology labs. At first, my relationship with Jane was good, she seemed upbeat and helpful. But it eventually deteriorated as I think the funding pressure on her coming from senior management began to build up.

Over time, I grew to resent the sloppy way the place was run. The head of the Institute was basically out of sight, rarely coming in and apparently taking little interest in the people doing the work. It seemed to me that my job kept changing with every new directive from Jane.

In the end, I was let go in July of 2019 along with several other people. Funding for the Institute was drying up. Grants were not coming in. I started applying for jobs immediately—in the Boston area and beyond. I came close to a few seemingly ideal jobs. But, in the end, I was passed over.

Each job application and the selection process that follows is an ordeal and itself almost a full-time job: checking every day for openings, working on different versions of my résumé, writing specific personal statements of interest that looked like they fit the job opening, going through an endless set of interviews, some in person, some by phone, and some by videoconference. And then the harrowing anxiety that builds up while waiting for the hiring decision to be made.

While looking for work, I took on some unpaid jobs. The first was as a marine science consultant for an organization in the Caribbean Islands called Beyond the Sea. I discovered the organization on the web and developed a working relationship with the people who started the venture. I helped them prepare a few grant proposals and did some SCUBA diving on various company operations. Before the pandemic, I was able to even spend some time on site in the Caribbean.

After Beyond the Sea, I took another unpaid, part-time job with the Ocean Mammal Rescue Center in northern California as an animal care and data intern. I found out about the internship from a state government website. One reason I took this gig was that I was told at the time a paid position might soon open up and I would be a good candidate. It was a small center—six people when I started—but had contacts and connections with the other rescue centers, research labs, and various coastal protection agencies up and down the coast. So I left Boston and moved across country in January 2020.

Then the pandemic hit full-on in March and the Center severely cut back its outreach programs and already small staff. The partial shutdown of the Center didn't affect me since I wasn't being paid. But it did cut down on the learning opportunities and the routine duties the internship allowed. Calls from citizens—the main source of our rescue opportunities—dropped way off; in part, a result of there being few beachgoers.

Looking back, however, I still consider it valuable experience. The project I worked on while there was to collect and analyze information from our own and other rescue centers in the state on the processes currently in use to inform best practices for stranded marine mammal care. I started from scratch and built out a data structure that I think is being used today. I was supervised on the project by Roxanne, who left the Center about five months after I started. She moved on to a bigger job with a statewide marine biology office in Sacramento. Since there was so little for me to do once my project was finished, I left about the same time as Roxanne, in August 2020.

I found my next job in September with a San Francisco–based Coastal Tides agency as an operations director. Thankfully, this was at last a paid position. The work involves a variety of tasks: managing a portfolio of environmental design and strategy projects, organizing meetings and webinars, helping with presentations, and almost anything else that comes up. It's all virtual, and I'm one of four current "partners" who do the work of the agency. I enjoy the work, but when I initially accepted, it was a part-time position, about 15 hours per week. At the time, my savings were dwindling down, and I needed a second job to cover my living expenses.

A second job soon materialized as a program fellow for the Ecosystem Funders Group (EFG). This too is part time, yet with worse pay and more hours (24 per week) than with Coastal Tides. It too is entirely virtual. I started with EFG in November of 2020. The job itself involves providing administrative and operational support to various marine conservation programs. I help plan and bring off virtual and in-person meetings (although there have been very few in-person meetings thus far). Basically, I try to get the diverse individuals and groups to interact with and understand one another—fishermen, academics, NGO members, marine researchers, and government people from, say, NOAA or the World Economic Forum.

What I like about virtual work is the autonomy and the personal time it affords me. I have lunch when I want, maybe walk the dog in the middle of the day, and I don't have to commute to work or dress a certain way. I can travel and take the work with me. I just spent six weeks visiting friends and family in Boston and New York while working my regular schedule (although it's harder than it sounds).

I really think I am far more productive working this way than in the office. I'm far more efficient and organized these days than I was at the university, where I was constantly being interrupted, really jerked around, subject to Jane's moods, and basically struggled to feel appreciated in a large organization.

A possible downside of remote work is that I've not formed any close relationships with coworkers in either the Coastal Tides Agency or the EFG. I pretty much work on my own, at my own pace in both places. There are some efforts to establish closer relations among the staff at EFG through virtual social hours a couple of times a month, but they haven't been very successful. At Coastal Tides, there are only three employees, and most of my contacts—aside from constant contact with the founding partner Anne—have been with clients and fishery people, who provide much of our data.

In April of 2022, Coastal Tides got great news. A grant proposal I worked on was approved. This is something we really didn't expect. We've been working on the proposal off and on since my first day on the job. The grant is for $450,000, and I will soon be a full-time employee as the operations director and lead project manager on the grant. My role with EFG will wind down over the next couple of months. This is a huge relief and a real opportunity for me to contribute to a cause that I care about.

The grant is for developing a data management system that helps support sustainable ocean resources. It's a big project. My job will remain virtual although there may be some future meetings face-to-face with collaborators. Data governance is not exactly a people-on-the-ground project, but it is important, and I've got some background in the work that's required. So a new chapter in my life opens up, one with good pay, some stability, and challenging work with interesting people.

In terms of my career, I've been surviving by taking on paid and unpaid work—with some help from the pandemic-related unemployment benefits. It's been a frustrating and anxiety-provoking period of stringing together various part-time gigs into something resembling full-time work. But I take some measure of satisfaction in having been able to do work that in some small way relates to my goal of creating a more sustainable marine environment.

Career Anchors and Growth Intentions Assessment

Given Maia's career transition following her master's degree in marine biology and her commitment to improving our marine environment, the strong extension toward Service in her Career Anchors line is as expected (see Exhibit 8.5 below). The values of a master's degree recipient in a technical field are also represented in the strong extension toward the Technical-Functional anchor. For Maia, Autonomy and Life-Work Integration are also prominent, which fits her career path to date.

There is a pattern in the Growth Intentions line that is a bit different and fascinating. Maia has indicated a strong interest in or need to be more Entrepreneurial. We can hazard a guess that this is related to Maia's focus on Autonomy and the implicit recognition that in the specialized field of publicly funded marine environment advocacy, Maia may be recognizing that knowing how to run an agency and creating buzz for a new endeavor demand skills and interests in entrepreneurship to some degree, and therefore she is

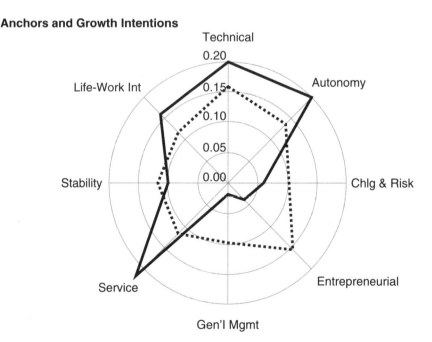

Anchors and Growth Intentions

Exhibit 8.5   Career Anchors and Growth Chart for Maia

recognizing the need to grow skills in this dimension. Another possibility is that Maia would be completely surprised by this pattern suggested by differences between the Career Anchors and the Growth Intentions lines. This illustrates why there is benefit to comparing all of these assessments, all of these items. These may be "false notes" for Maia, they might also be crystal clear insights, leanings that she might not have articulated in an interview but for which she could become increasingly confident and driven.

Career Anchors and Growth Intentions for You

If you go through the Career Anchors and Growth Intentions exercises and are not surprised at all, seeing just what you expect of yourself, reward yourself for your self-awareness, and focus on finding ways to communicate this self-assurance without it coming across as horribly arrogant.

For the rest of you who go through the exercise and learn something new about yourself that you either want to feature in your career journey or want to get over and move beyond, we hope the items and the charts are helpful insight generators. This is the end goal—whether validating or challenging to your sense of self, we hope the insight makes it easier for you to handle the next tough interview question or the "fork in the road."

9

Conclusion

WE WILL LEAVE you with Robert Frost's "The Road Not Taken" (1915):

> Two roads diverged in a yellow wood,
> And sorry I could not travel both
> And be one traveler, long I stood
> And looked down one as far as I could
> To where it bent in the undergrowth;
>
> Then took the other, as just as fair,
> And having perhaps the better claim,
> Because it was grassy and wanted wear;
> Though as for that the passing there
> Had worn them really about the same,
>
> And both that morning equally lay
> In leaves no step had trodden black.
> Oh, I kept the first for another day!
> Yet knowing how way leads on to way,
> I doubted if I should ever come back.
>
> I shall be telling this with a sigh
> Somewhere ages and ages hence:
> Two roads diverged in a wood, and I—
> I took the one less traveled by,
> And that has made all the difference.

We join the many who revere this poem's implications for career journeys and career choices. It seems to bolster our sense of individual choice and self-determination. Taking "the one less traveled by" is a hard decision that, as this traveler says, "has made all of the difference." This sure sounds like an encouragement to go your own way, don't follow the trodden path, be autonomous and entrepreneurial. What a poetic validation of that courageous career choice that makes all of the difference!

And yet there is another reading! We will not pretend to know what Frost had in mind. Still, in the words themselves there is the peril and ambivalence we feel about career choices. We all know the unlikelihood we will "ever come back." Perhaps this is why Frost's traveler will tell "with a sigh" about the choice. Does a career traveler ever tell us of a great successful decision she or he made "with a sigh"? Is it possible that Frost's traveler is hinting that "all the difference" was not all good? Or even implying that taking the road not taken was a mistake? Tough fork-in-the-road career decisions can certainly yield mistakes *for which we sigh* and later rationalize, "No regrets, it is what it is. . . ."

You cannot go back in time and redo a career decision. As all career decisions are consequential, you might need a better reason to follow the less trodden path than the perilous allure that it is simply less trodden.

As a metaphorical career seeker, Frost's traveler would also be unusual in that he or she *was alone* in the fateful choice of path. Careers are webs of relationships. As our five career anchors stories emphasize, the choices our seekers made were deeply relational, cast by the influences of other people, not just the leanings of the career seeker alone. Does it now make sense why we started (Chapter Two) with relationship mapping? It would be a very strange world indeed if we could make career decisions in a vacuum, without the compelling influences of personal and professional connections. In his infinite wisdom, Dr. Seuss (Theodore Geisel) reminds us to not forget the "many strange birds" we will encounter as we go. We need "strange birds" to attract us and to repel us in making work and life decisions. Realistically we will not find the untaken career road without the relationships that got us to the two diverging paths in the first place.

If you go through career assessments, perhaps including career anchors and growth intentions, you may find it much easier to handle that tricky fork in the road such that the choice you make is because it aligns affirmatively with your relationships, past and present, and your intentions for future growth. This could make all the difference in a positive way—you can take the path others have not taken because it all lines up for you and those around you in ways that it may not have for others. In the end, the correct decision finds the best path, whether or not it is the other path.

It never hurts to ask for help and to tap into the tools and resources that provide insights to help you reach moments of clarity. You can be confident of career choices, with no regretful "sighs," when you have sought the right information to become mindful, reflective, holistic, and honest with yourself in all of your career moments of truth.

APPENDIX

Career Anchors and Career-Oriented Personality Assessments

CAREER COUNSELING HAS become a major field in the last fifty years and is filled with various kinds of tools, surveys, programs, and workshops that promise you not only self-insight but, in some cases, even a job at the end of the program. The career anchors work started with the research panel that Ed Schein launched in the early 1960s but did not produce any useful research results until the 1970s when revisiting the panel members revealed this concept of career anchors and helped to define concepts and work-shops for mid-career adults to supplement the already massive programs that were present for those just beginning their careers.

Apart from the research results on the importance of anchors as an aspect of mid and later careers, Ed discovered that the research interviews were received by everyone as a unique experience of self-discovery. Almost everyone said, after the experience how "this is the first time that anyone has ever asked me this question, so for the first time I am thinking about my work and my career."

It was this insight that led to evolving the booklet and the exercises that went through four editions in the last 40 years and is now confronting an entirely different world because of technological and social changes, as well as the impact of the pandemic. The point is that there is today not only much more help available to the mid-career occupant but an even greater need for such help as the world of work has become more volatile and complex.

We cannot possibly review all that is available, but we feel that two concepts are now so widely used that it is worth commenting on how they relate to *Career Anchors*—The Clifton *StrengthsFinder 2.0* (2007) and the Myers-Briggs Type Indicator (MBTI).

Career Anchors and *StrengthsFinder 2.0* (aka CliftonStrengths)

The CliftonStrengths assessment was developed by Don Clifton to help managers, leaders, job seekers, and others to develop self-insight and self-awareness about what they can "bring to the table." More information is available at https://www.gallup.com/cliftonstrengths/en/252137/home.aspx.

What are an individuals' personality characteristics that should be featured or will be visible in interactions with other people, particularly in interview or influence interactions? CliftonStrengths is not focused on helping you address or answer to your weaknesses, nor is it about helping you appear "well-rounded." It is about your five or more key strengths. If I know my "CliftonStrengths," I can more persuasively, if not authentically, represent who I am and how and why I can add value.

In this sense, CliftonStrengths is very much complementary with *Career Anchors*. Still, there is a core difference between the two models—*Career Anchors* reflect how and why we have made our career choices. Our personality and preferences factor into these decisions, as do many other factors. CliftonStrengths does not necessarily assume one has a multiyear base of career decisions to tap into for self-insight. In this sense anchors and strengths in combination provide a richer view, a richer dimensionality to self-insight that you can bring to the early career job search, mid-career pivot, or encore career remake.

To have a sense of how CliftonStrengths and *Career Anchors* might relate to each other or map to each other, the following table lists strengths and the anchors that may well be associated with the personality characteristic. This association is anecdotal and layered—any individual will have multiple CliftonStrengths just as they will have prominent anchors and unimportant anchors. Our list below includes a couple anchors that we would expect to be associated with each of the CliftonStrengths; we will leave it up to the reader to fill in the picture of all of the strengths and anchors. In the end, the goal is more insight and self-awareness gained by looking at the assessments side by side.

Table A.1   CliftonStrengths and Career Anchors

CliftonStrength	Related Career Anchor 1	Related Career Anchor 2
Achiever	Entrepreneurial	Technical-Functional
Activator	Autonomy	Entrepreneurial
Adaptability	Autonomy	Challenge and Risk
Analytical	Technical-Functional	
Arranger	General Management	Challenge and Risk
Belief	Service	Life-Work Integration
Command	General Management	Entrepreneurial
Communication	Entrepreneurial	Technical-Functional
Competition	General Management	Technical-Functional
Connectedness	Service	General Management
Consistency	Stability	Service
Context	Technical-Functional	Life-Work Integration
Deliberative	General Management	Stability
Developer	Service	Autonomy
Discipline	Technical-Functional	Stability
Empathy	Service	General Management
Focus	Entrepreneurial	Autonomy
Futuristic	Technical-Functional	Autonomy
Harmony	Service	Life-Work Integration
Ideation	Technical-Functional	Challenge and Risk
Includer	Service	General Management
Individualization	Autonomy	Service
Input	Service	Technical-Functional
Intellection	Technical-Functional	Life-Work Integration
Learner	Technical-Functional	Autonomy
Maximizer	General Management	Life-Work Integration
Positivity	Entrepreneurial	Challenge and Risk
Relator	Life-Work Integration	Entrepreneurial
Responsibility	Autonomy	Stability

Table A.1   (*Continued*)

CliftonStrength	Related Career Anchor 1	Related Career Anchor 2
Restorative	Service	Technical-Functional
Self-Assurance	Entrepreneurial	Challenge and Risk
Significance	Autonomy	General Management
Strategic	Technical-Functional	Challenge and Risk
Woo	General Management	Life-Work Integration

Career Anchors and the Myers-Briggs Type Indicator (aka MBTI)

MBTI is another very popular and common personality assessment for first-time job seekers all the way through to very high-level executive candidates. It is worthwhile reading about the history and current use of the assessment for individuals and teams at https://www.themyersbriggs .com/en-US.

This assessment keys off four polarities: (1) extroversion vs. introversion; (2) How people gather information, sensing (facts) vs. intuition (patterns); (3) How people tend to make decisions based on gathered data, thinking (factual) vs. feeling (emotional); and (4) How people process the world around them through, judging (structure in categories) vs. perceiving (unstructured and open).

The MBTI assessment then bundles the four dimensions such that there are 4×4 combinations, that is, 16 patterns of personality to which colorful descriptors are assigned. Once again, in the spirit of layering insights on insights, consider these loose associations of MBTI and *Career Anchors*:

Table A.2   Myers-Briggs Categories and Career Anchors

MBTI Category	Career Anchor	Explanation
Introvert (I)	Autonomy	*Thriving alone*
Extrovert (E)	General Management	*In front of people*
Sensing (S)	Challenge and Risk	*Facts against odds*
Intuiting (N)	Entrepreneurial	*Seeing patterns, trends*
Thinking (T)	Technical-Functional	*Facts to be accumulated*
Feeling (F)	Life-Work Integration	*Holistic, how things feel*
Judging (J)	Stability	*Keeping things orderly*
Perceiving (P)	Service	*Perceiving what's needed*

There is no doubt that this mapping of anchors to MBTI could be debated, shifted around with good arguments supporting changes. MBTI is, nonetheless, used as a clustering—it says little about who you are to know that you are an introvert. It says a lot more to know that you are an INTP or ENTJ. This would suggest that if you are an INTP, your anchors would show preferences for Autonomy, Entrepreneurial, Technical-Functional, and Service. It turns out this is pretty close, and where it gets a bit muddy for you may be between "thinking" and "feeling" and between "Technical-Functional" and "Life-Work Integration." So perhaps the mapping is not exact. Regardless, you may learn more about yourself when comparing *Career Anchors* to MBTI and notice some discrepancies or head scratchers.

In the table below, we list the MBTI characteristics and their descriptors and suggest which career anchors may map into these 16 personality types. These 16 personality types are described in detail on The Myers-Briggs Company (formerly CPP, Inc) website, at https://www.themyersbriggs .com/en-US/Resources/MBTI-Shareables.

Again, as a personality assessment the MBTI can apply to any adult, whether newly graduated from college or about to retire. *Career Anchors*, as we have said, may not provide as much help to a career seeker with no job experience. For an early career or mid-career seeker, on the other hand, the mapping of MBTI to Career Anchors patterns could be quite illuminating, whether reinforcing or challenging of career patterns or career choices. In that spirit, let's take this proposed mapping and cluster it alongside the MBTI clusters and descriptors:

Table A.3   MBTI 16 Types and Related Career Anchors

MBTI "type"	Related Career Anchors
"Responsible Realist"	Autonomy
Introvert	Challenge and Risk
Sensing	Technical-Functional
Thinking	Stability
Judging	
"Logical Pragmatist"	Autonomy
Introvert	Challenge and Risk
Sensing	Technical-Functional
Thinking	Service
Perceiver	
"Practical Helper"	Autonomy
Introvert	Challenge and Risk
Sensing	Life-Work Integration
Feeling	Stability
Judging	
"Versatile Supporter"	Autonomy
Introvert	Challenge and Risk
Sensing	Life-Work Integration
Feeling	Service
Perceiving	

(continued)

Table A.3   (Continued)

MBTI "type"	Related Career Anchors
"Insightful Visionary"	Autonomy
Introvert	Entrepreneurial
Intuiting(N)	Life-Work Integration
Feeling	Stability
Judging	
"Thoughtful Idealist"	Autonomy
Introvert	Entrepreneurial
Intuiting(N)	Life-Work Integration
Feeling	Service
Perceiving	
"Conceptual Planner"	Autonomy
Introvert	Entrepreneurial
Intuiting(N)	Technical-Functional
Thinking	Stability
Judging	
"Objective Analyst"	Autonomy
Introvert	Entrepreneurial
Intuiting(N)	Technical-Functional
Thinking	Service
Perceiving	
"Energetic Problem-solver"	General Management
Extrovert	Challenge and Risk
Sensing	Technical-Functional
Thinking	Service
Perceiving	
"Efficient Organizer"	General Management
Extrovert	Challenge and Risk
Sensing	Technical-Functional
Thinking	Stability
Judging	

Table A.3 (Continued)

MBTI "type"	Related Career Anchors
"Enthusiastic Improviser"	General Management
Extrovert	Challenge and Risk
Sensing	Life-Work Integration
Feeling	Service
Perceiving	
"Supportive Contributor"	General Management
Extrovert	Challenge and Risk
Sensing	Life-Work Integration
Feeling	Stability
Judging	
"Imaginative Motivator"	General Management
Extrovert	Entrepreneurial
Intuiting(N)	Life-Work Integration
Feeling	Service
Perceiving	
"Compassionate Facilitator"	General Management
Extrovert	Entrepreneurial
Intuiting(N)	Life-Work Integration
Feeling	Stability
Judging	
"Enterprising Explorer"	General Management
Extrovert	Entrepreneurial
Intuiting(N)	Technical-Functional
Thinking	Service
Perceiving	
"Decisive Strategist"	General Management
Extrovert	Entrepreneurial
Intuiting(N)	Technical-Functional
Thinking	Stability
Judging	

This is not exact science, by any stretch of the imagination. It is a triangulation, another angle on things. For those readers who know their MBTI type the career anchors should align to some extent with the MBTI descriptors. And that could be validating or thought-provoking and ultimately insight generating.

One of the authors was once told that "almost all of the VPs and C-levels at this company are ENTJ". It was an odd statement as it suggested little diversity in a management team that was demonstrably more diverse, and it implied a bit of a normative bent that could be quite constrictive in succession planning. "We can only promote ENTJs" would not be the most inclusive way to think about building and then tapping a "strong bench." With the *Career Anchor* triangulation, it would nevertheless make some sense that the best candidates to take over senior leadership were those who had made career choices along the way that leaned toward "General Management," "Entrepreneurship," "Technical-Functional" expertise, and "Stability." This was a maturing technology company. In that light, the MBTI mapping to *Career Anchors* shows a nice alignment between personality types and career anchor optimizations fit for this company at this stage of maturity.

This triangulation made sense, and if readers find some alignment like this for themselves it's reinforcing and empowering. If the opposite is true, the triangulation makes no sense at all, there will still be insight to be gleaned from the gaps. Why is there no alignment? Is it possible it is in the assessment instruments themselves? Again, this is not an exact science. It may also be that one can make career choices that do not always align with personality traits. Either way, this is a powerful insight to have at any stage of a career journey.

Research Notes and References

Chapter One

The twenty reflections are based roughly on the last decade's worth of writing and research on the broad economic and social shifts that affect work and organization. The focus is on change in workplace practices that seemingly have significant effect on our personal and collective lives. These shifts play out not only in the United States but globally, albeit at different rates and emphasis, as well. The list includes both prescriptive or normative writings and empirically based trend studies. Organized by the three categories we used to highlight the changes, representative works examining mostly—but not exclusively—the trends in the United States include:

New Ways of Working:

1. Stephen R. Barley and Gideon Kunda, *Gurus, Hired Guns and Warm Bodies: Itinerant Experts in the Knowledge Economy*. Princeton, NJ: Princeton University Press, 2006.

139

2. Peter Cappelli, *The Future of the Office: Work from Home, Remote Work, and the Hard Choices We All Face*. Philadelphia: Wharton School Press, 2021.
3. Amy Edmondson, *The Fearless Organization: Creating Psychological Safety in the Workplace for Learning, Innovation and Growth*. San Francisco: Wiley, 2018.
4. Matthew E. Kahn, *Going Remote: How the Flexible Work Economy Can Improve Our Lives and Our Cities*. Berkeley, CA: University of California Press, 2022.
5. Leslie Perlow, *Sleeping with Your Cell Phone: How to Break the 24/7 Habit and Change the Way You Work*. Boston: Harvard Business School Press, 2012.
6. Sanjay Rishi, Benjamin Breslau, and Peter Miscovich, *The Workplace You Need Now*. San Francisco: Wiley, 2021.
7. Alex Rosenblat, *Uberland: How Algorithms Are Rewriting the Rules of work*. Berkeley, CA: University of California Press, 2018.

New Organizational Realities:

8. Stephen R. Barley, Beth A. Bechky, and Frances J. Milliken, "The Changing Nature of Work: Careers, Identities and Work Lives in the 21st Century," *Academy of Management Discoveries*, 3(2): 111–115, 2017.
9. Victor Tan Chen, *Cut Loose: Jobless and Hopeless in an Unfair Economy*. Berkeley: University of California Press, 2015.
10. Christine M. Beckman and Melissa Mazmanian, *Dreams of the Overworked: Living, Working & Parenting in the Digital Age*. Stanford, CA: Stanford University Press, 2020.
11. David Burkus, *Leading from Anywhere: The Essential Guide to Managing Remote Teams*. Boston: Mariner Books, 2021.
12. Gerald F. Davis, *The Vanishing American Corporation: Navigating the Hazards of a New Economy*. Oakland, CA: Berrett-Koehler, 2016.
13. Douglas T. Hall, *Careers In and Out of Organizations*. Thousand Oaks, CA: Sage, 2002.

14. Erin Kelly, *Overload: How Good Jobs Went Bad and What We Can Do About It.* Princeton, NJ: Princeton University Press, 2021.
15. Tom Kochan and Lee Dyer, *Shaping the Future of Work.* New York: Routledge, 2020.
16. Paul Osterman and Barbara Dyer, *Creating Good Jobs: An Industry Based Strategy.* Cambridge, MA: MIT Press, 2020.
17. Jeff Schwartz, *Work Disrupted: Opportunity, Resilience, and Growth in the Accelerated Future of Work.* NY: Wiley, 2021.
18. Farah Stockman, *American Made: What Happens to People When Work Disappears.* NY: Random House, 2022.
19. Catherine Turco, *The Conversational Firm: Rethinking Bureaucracy on the Age of Social Media.* NY: Columbia University Press, 2016.

Global Turbulence:

20. Edward Aldwen, *Failure to Adjust: How Americans Got Left Behind in the Global Economy.* Lanham, MD: Rowman & Littlefield, 2017.
21. Erik Brynjolfsson and Andrew McAfee, *Race against the Machine: How the Digital Revolution is Accelerating Innovation, Driving Productivity, and Irreversibly Transforming Employment and the Economy.* NY: Digital Frontier Press, 2012.
22. Anne Case and Angus Deaton, *Deaths of Despair and the Future of Capitalism.* Princeton, NJ: Princeton University Press, 2020.
23. Hugh Guntz, Mila Lazarova, and Wolfgang Mayrhofer (eds.), *The Routledge Companion to Career Studies.* London: Routledge, 2019.
24. Tsedal Neeley, *Remote Work Revolution: Succeeding from Anywhere.* NY: Harper Business, 2021.
25. Michael J. Sandel, *The Tyranny of Merit: What's Become of the Common Good?* NY: Farrar, Straus and Giroux, 2020.

Chapter Two

The literature on building (and sustaining) relationships of various types is vast. The model presented in this chapter rests on work that Ed Schein first published in [1] and further elaborated in [2]. It draws on some related work by [3]–[6]. An earlier version of relationship mapping and career anchors—then labeled job/role mapping—is found in [7]

1. Edgar H. Schein, *Humble Consulting: How to Provide Real Help Faster*. Oakland, California: Brett-Koehler Publishers, 2016.
2. Edgar H. Schein and Peter A. Schein, *Humble Leadership: The Power of Relationships, Openness and Trust*. Oakland, California: Brett-Koehler Publishers, 2018.
3. William Isaacs, *Dialogue*. NY: Doubleday Currency, 1999.
4. Amy C. Edmundson, *Teaming: How Organizations Learn, Innovate and Compete in the Knowledge Economy*. San Francisco: Jossey-Bass, 2012.
5. Jodi H. Gittell, *Transforming Relationships for High Performance: The Power of Relational Coordination*. Stanford, CA: Stanford University Press, 2016.
6. Peter Senge, *The Fifth Discipline*. NY: Doubleday, 1990.
7. Edgar H. Schein and John Van Maanen, "Career Anchors and Job/Role Planning. Tools for Career and Talent Management." *Organizational Dynamics*. 45(1): 165–173, 2016.

Chapters Three and Four

The distinction of the external and internal career comes from Ed Schein's original research [1]. A more detailed and extended treatment of career anchors is presented in [2] and in Edgar H. Schein's two articles in later decades [3] and [4].

Some of the analytic groundings for career studies are found in [5] and [6]. The most recent and extensive treatment of career anchors is found in the participants workbook of Edgar H. Schein and John Van Maanen [7]. Our description of the eight anchors draws on this source.

1. Edgar H. Schein, "Career anchors and career paths: A panel Study of management school graduates" In John Van Maanen (ed.) *Organizational Careers: Some New Perspectives*, San Francisco; Wiley, 49–64, 1977.
2. Edgar H. Schein, *Career Dynamics: Matching Individual and Organizational Needs.* Reading, MA: Addison-Wesley, 1978.
3. Edgar H. Schein, "Individuals and Careers." In Jay Lorsch (ed.) *Handbook of Organizational Behavior.* Englewood Cliffs, NJ: Prentice-Hall, 80–88, 1987.
4. Edgar H. Schein, "Career Anchors Revisited: Implications for Career Development in the 21st Century" *Academy of Management Executive*, 10, 80–88, 1996.
5. John Van Maanen, "Experiencing organization: Notes on the meaning of careers and socialization," In John Van Maanen (eds.), *Organizational Careers: Some New Perspectives*. NY: Wiley, 15–48, 1977.
6. John Van Maanen and Stephen Barley, "Occupational Communities: Culture and Control in Organizations," In Barry M. Staw, and Larry L. Cummings (eds.), *Research in Organizational Behavior*. Greenwich, CT: JAI Press, 287–365, 1984.
7. Edgar H. Schein and John Van Maanen, *Career Anchors: The Changing Nature of Work and Careers*, 4th edition. San Francisco: Wiley, 2013.

About the Authors

Ed Schein (1928–2023) was Professor Emeritus of the Massachusetts Institute of Te-chnology (MIT) Sloan School of Man-agement. He was edu-cated at the University of Chicago, Stanford University, and Harvard University, where he received his PhD in social psychology (1952). He worked at the Walter Reed Institute of Research for four years and then joined MIT, where he taught until 2005. He has published extensively—*Organizational Psychology, 3rd Edition* (1980); *Process Consultation Revisited* (1999); *Career Dynamics*

(1978); *Career Anchors*, *4th Edition*, with John Van Maanen (2013); *Organizational Culture and Leadership*, *5th Edition* (2017); and *The Corporate Culture Survival Guide*, *3rd Edition*, with Peter Schein (2019). In 2009 he published *Helping*, a book on the general theory and practice of giving and receiving help followed by *Humble Inquiry* (2013) and, working with his son Peter, published *Humble Leadership* (2018) and a second edition of *Humble Inquiry* (2021). He was the 2009 recipient of the Distinguished Scholar-Practitioner Award of the Academy of Management, the 2012 recipient of the Lifetime Achievement Award from the International Leadership Association, the 2015 Lifetime Achievement Award in Organization Development from the International OD Network, and held an honorary doctorate from the IEDC Bled School of Management in Slovenia.

John Van Maanen is the Erwin H. Schell Professor Emeritus at the MIT Sloan School of Management. He is an ethnographer of organizations ranging in type from police organizations to educational institutions, as well as a variety of business firms. Cultural descriptions figure prominently in his studies of such diverse work worlds as beat patrolmen on city streets in the United States; police detectives and their guv'nors in London; fishermen in the North Atlantic; and park operatives in the Sistine Chapel of Fakery, Disneyland (here and abroad). He has taught at MIT Sloan since 1972 and has been a visiting professor at Yale University, University of Surrey, INSEAD, and is an Honorary Fellow at Cambridge University. He is the author of numerous books and articles including *Tales of the Field, 2nd Edition* (2011), and *Career Anchors, 4th Edition*, with Ed Schein (2013). John was educated at California State University, Long Beach, and University of California, Irvine (PhD 1972).

Peter Schein is the cofounder of the Organizational Culture and Leadership Institute (OCLI. org), which is dedicated to advancing organizational development and design through a deeper understanding of organizational culture and leadership theory. Peter's writing draws on over thirty years of industry experience in product marketing and corporate development at tech-nology pioneers including Pacific Bell, Apple, Silicon Graphics, Inc., Packeteer (BlueCoat), and Sun Microsystems, Inc. (Oracle), with a focus on the underlying organizational culture challenges that growth engenders in innovation-driven enterprises.

He is coauthor of four books with Ed Schein, including *Humble Leadership* (2018), *The Corporate Culture Survival Guide, 3rd Edition*, and their most recent release, *Humble Inquiry, 2nd Edition* (2021). Peter was educated at Stanford University and Northwestern/Kellogg (MBA 1991).

Index